Easy-Does-It Grammar
for Grades 4-12

by

Mary A. Lombardo

LINWORTH
LEARNING

Activities & Resources
From the Minds of Teachers

Library of Congress Cataloging-in-Publication Data

Lombardo, Mary A.
  Easy-does-it grammar for grades 4-12 / Mary A. Lombardo.
      p. cm.
  Includes index.
  ISBN 1-58683-213-1 (pbk.)
  1. English language--Grammar--Study and teaching (Elementary) 2. English language--Grammar--Study and teaching (Secondary) 3. Language arts (Elementary) 4. Language arts (Secondary) I. Title.
  LB1576.L626 2007
  428'.0071--dc22
                              2006026939

Published by Linworth Publishing, Inc.
480 East Wilson Bridge Road, Suite L
Worthington, Ohio 43085

1-58683-196-8

5 4 3 2 1

Table of Contents

About the Author v

Overview v

Teacher Introduction vi

Organization of the Book vi

Objectives vi

Correlation with NCTE Standards vi

How to Use This Book vii

Section One: Parts of Speech 1

   Lesson 1: Common & Proper Nouns 3
      Common & Proper Nouns Teacher Information 3
      Common & Proper Nouns Pre and Post Test 3
      Common & Proper Nouns Activities 4
      Student Handout 1: Common Nouns 5
      Student Handout 2: Proper Nouns 6
   Lesson 2: Singular & Plural Nouns 7
      Singular & Plural Nouns Teacher Information 7
      Singular & Plural Nouns Pre and Post Test 8
      Singular & Plural Nouns Activities 8
      Student Handout 3: Singular & Plural Regular Nouns 9
      Student Handout 4: Singular & Plural Irregular Nouns 10
   Lesson 3: Possessive Nouns 11
      Possessive Nouns Teacher Information 11
      Possessive Nouns Pre and Post Test 11
      Possessive Nouns Activities 12
      Student Handout 5: Possessive Nouns 13
   Review, Lessons 1 through 3 14
   Lesson 4: Personal Pronouns 15
      Personal Pronouns Teacher Information 15
      Personal Pronouns Pre and Post Test 16
      Personal Pronouns Activities 17
      Student Handout 6: Personal Pronouns 18
   Lesson 5: Indefinite Pronouns 19
      Indefinite Pronouns Teacher Information 19
      Indefinite Pronouns Pre and Post Test 19
      Indefinite Pronouns Activities 20
      Student Handout 7: Indefinite Pronouns 21
   Lesson 6: Possessive Pronouns 22
      Possessive Pronouns Teacher Information 22
      Possessive Pronouns Pre and Post Test 22
      Possessive Pronouns Activities 23
      Student Handout 8: Possessive Pronouns 24

Table of Contents continued

Lesson 7: Adjectives..25
    Adjectives Teacher Information...25
    Adjectives Pre and Post Test 25
    Adjectives Activities 26
    Student Handout 9: Adjectives One...27
    Student Handout 10: Adjectives Two...28
Review, Lessons 4 through 7 29
Lesson 8: Verbs 31
    Verbs Teacher Information...31
    Verbs Pre and Post Test 32
    Verbs Activities 32
    Student Handout 11: Verbs 33
Lesson 9: Forming Verb Tenses 34
    Forming Verb Tenses Teacher Information 34
    Forming Verb Tenses Pre and Post Test..34
    Forming Verb Tenses Activities 35
    Student Handout 12: Forming Verb Tenses 36
Lesson 10: Present, Past, and Future Perfect Verbs 37
    Present, Past, and Future Perfect Verbs Teacher Information 37
    Present, Past, and Future Perfect Verbs Pre and Post Test 37
    Present, Past, and Future Perfect Verbs Activities 38
    Student Handout 13: Present, Past, and Future Perfect Verbs 39
Lesson 11: Active and Passive Verbs 40
    Active and Passive Verbs Teacher Information 40
    Active and Passive Verbs Pre and Post Test......................................41
    Active and Passive Verbs Activities 41
    Student Handout 14: Active and Passive Verbs 42
Review, Lessons 8 through 11 43
Lesson 12: Adverbs 44
    Adverbs Teacher Information 44
    Adverbs Pre and Post Test 45
    Adverbs Activities 45
    Student Handout 15: Adverbs 46
Lesson 13: Complements 47
    Complements Teacher Information 47
    Complements Pre and Post Test..48
    Complements Activities 48
    Student Handout 16: Complements 49
Review, Lessons 12 through 13 50
Lesson 14: Prepositions 51
    Prepositions Teacher Information 51
    Prepositions Pre and Post Test..52
    Prepositions Activities 52
    Student Handout 17: Prepositions 53

Table of Contents continued

Lesson 15: Conjunctions 54
    Conjunctions Teacher Information...54
    Conjunctions Pre and Post Test 55
    Conjunctions Activities 55
    Student Handout 18: Conjunctions 56
Lesson 16: Interjections 57
    Interjections Teacher Information 57
    Interjections Pre and Post Test...57
    Interjections Activities 58
    Student Handout 19: Interjections 59
Review, Lessons 14 through 16 60

Section Two: Punctuation 61

Lesson 17: Sentence Beginnings and Endings.....................................63
    Sentence Beginnings and Endings Teacher Information 63
    Sentence Beginnings and Endings Pre and Post Test 63
    Sentence Beginnings and Endings Activities................................64
    Student Handout 20: Sentence Beginnings and Endings.................65
Lesson 18: The Comma 66
    The Comma Teacher Information 66
    The Comma Pre and Post Test...67
    The Comma Activities 67
    Student Handout 21: The Comma, One.....................................68
    Student Handout 22: The Comma, Two 69
Lesson 18: The Apostrophe 70
    The Apostrophe Teacher Information 70
    The Apostrophe Pre and Post Test 71
    The Apostrophe Activities 71
    Student Handout 23: The Apostrophe 72
Review, Lessons Seventeen through Nineteen......................................73
Lesson 20: Colons and Semicolons 74
    Colons and Semicolons Teacher Information 74
    Colons and Semicolons Pre and Post Test.................................74
    Colons and Semicolons Activities 75
    Student Handout 24: Colons 76
    Student Handout 25: Semicolons...77
Lesson 21: Quotation Marks 78
    Quotation Marks Teacher Information...78
    Quotation Marks Pre and Post Test 79
    Quotation Marks Activities 79
    Student Handout 26: Quotation Marks 80
    Student Handout 27: Quotation Marks Punctuation 81
Review, Lessons 20 through 21 82

Table of Contents continued

Section Three: Putting It All Together 83

    Lesson 22: Sentences 85

        Sentences Teacher Information 85

        Sentences Pre and Post Test..85

        Sentences Activities 86

        Student Handout 28: Sentences 87

    Lesson 23: Simple, Complete, and Compound Subjects and Predicates 88

        Simple, Complete, and Compound Subjects and Predicates

            Teacher Information 88

        Simple, Complete, and Compound Subjects and Predicates Pre and Post Test 89

        Simple, Complete, and Compound Subjects and Predicates Activities 89

        Student Handout 29: Simple, Complete, and Compound Subjects 90

        Student Handout 30: Simple, Complete, and Compound Predicates 91

    Lesson 24: Phrases, Clauses, and Complex Sentences 92

        Phrases, Clauses, and Complex Sentences Teacher Information...........................92

        Phrases, Clauses, and Complex Sentences Pre and Post Test 93

        Phrases, Clauses, and Complex Sentences Activities 93

        Student Handout 31: Phrases, Clauses, and Complex Sentences 94

    Review, Lessons 22 through 24 95

    Lesson Twenty-Five: Using Modifiers...96

        Using Modifiers Teacher Information 96

        Using Modifiers Pre and Post Test 97

        Using Modifiers Activities 97

        Student Handout 32: Using Modifiers..98

    Lesson 26: Run-on Sentences and Fragments 99

        Run-on Sentences and Fragments Teacher Information 99

        Run-on Sentences and Fragments Pre and Post Test.......................................100

        Run-on Sentences and Fragments Activities 100

        Student Handout 33: Run-on Sentences and Fragments 101

    Review, Lessons 25 through 26 102

Student Handout Table of Contents 103

Index 104

About the Author

Mary A. Lombardo is a retired teacher who has taught all grade levels from first through sixth grade including several years in an alternative school setting teaching the combined grades and four years as a reading teacher. Her undergraduate degree is in elementary education, and she holds a Master of Arts degree in education with a minor in English and drama. She is the author of seven Linworth books for teachers on a variety of subjects

Overview

So often, people think of English grammar as hard to understand, and that is because sometimes it is! The purpose of this book is to present the rules of grammar in a way that makes it easy and enjoyable for the learner to understand and use good grammar. A basic introduction to English grammar, the book encompasses parts of speech, punctuation, capitalization, and sentence structure. The instruction is appropriate for students in grades four through junior high, ESL students, and basic English classes at the high school level.

Teacher Introduction

Organization of the Book

This book is divided into three sections: Parts of Speech, Punctuation and Capitalization, and Putting it All Together in Sentences.

The sections are divided into lessons that include a teacher information sheet, a pre and post test, a list of suggested activities that can serve as lesson plans to introduce and teach the subject matter, and at least one student handout. There are 25 lessons in all and 42 student handouts, nine of which are cumulative review handouts.

Because the student handouts for the lessons contain information as well as practice exercises, if collated, they can serve as a grammar handbook for the students. A separate table of contents for the student handbook is included after the last lesson.

Objectives

1. Provide a basic introduction to English grammar;

2. Present the rules of grammar in a way that makes it easy and enjoyable for the learner to understand and use good grammar;

3. Identify parts of speech and the rules of punctuation and capitalization;

4. Show how sentences are structured;

5. Provide practice in using rules of grammar.

Correlation with NCTE Standards

The National Council of Teachers of English has developed 12 standards citing how students should be helped to develop appropriate language skills. The subject matter, activities, and student handouts in this book provide students the opportunity to become familiar with the use of language structure and conventions and help teachers incorporate NCTE standards into their curriculum. The complete list of standards can be found at http://www.ncte.com.

How to Use This Book

The teacher can choose to use this book in several different ways.

1. Use the pretest to determine if the entire lesson needs to be taught and to help choose which of the suggested activities to use.

2. Start at the beginning of the book and go through all the lessons and handouts for a quick review of basic English grammar for older students.

3. Gather a small group of students together who are having difficulty with a specific skill and do a mini-lesson with the group.

4. For ESL, special education, basic English classes, and younger students, use this book as an introduction to grammar by going through each lesson thoroughly and, if needed, providing further instruction and practice. For these students, knowing the names of parts of speech is not as important as being able to use the parts of speech.

5. The lessons and activities can be presented to the entire class. Then cooperative groups can complete the handouts together, discussing and agreeing on reasons for correct answers.

6. The lessons do not have to be presented in the order listed. Teachers can present the lessons in the order that best suits their needs.

7. Collect and collate all handouts so the students will each have a grammar handbook of their own. Just before the index in this book, there is a copy-ready "Table of Contents" for the handouts.

8. Administer a post test. Re-teach the lesson, if needed, to the entire class or to select students who need the extra instruction.

SECTION ONE
Parts of Speech

nouns
pronouns
verbs
adverbs
adjectives
complements
prepositions
conjunctions
interjections

Lesson 1 Common and Proper Nouns

Common & Proper Nouns Teacher Information

Subjects and Predicates: All sentences are made up of two main parts, a subject and a predicate. The most important part of the subject is the noun, the person or thing that is talked about in the sentence, and the most important part of the predicate is the verb, the word that shows physical (run) or mental (believe) action. This lesson is about nouns or naming words.

Definitions
A **noun** is the name of a person, place, or thing.

A **common noun** is the name of a general person, place, or thing, and is not capitalized. Examples: *girl, boy, city, zoo, book, straw, honesty, love.*

A **proper noun** is the name of a specific person, place, or thing, and is always capitalized. Examples: *James, Mrs. Chavez, California, Bronx Zoo, Ford, Nike.*

Concrete nouns refer to tangibles like *girl, egg,* and *picture.*

Abstract nouns refer to ideas or qualities such as *honor, love,* and *hatred.*

Determining Part of Speech
Whether a word is a noun or some other part of speech is determined by how the word is used in a sentence. For example, "*name*" is a noun in the sentence, "*Her name is Marcia.*"

It is a verb in the sentence, "*The principal will name the winner of the spelling bee.*"

If a word is used to name a person, place, or thing, it serves as a noun.

☑ Common & Proper Nouns Pre and Post Test

Follow the instructions below.

Define a noun. _____

_____

Circle the common nouns and underline the proper nouns in the sentences below.

Bart washed Mrs. Perea's car. She paid him enough money to take his friend Anna to the movies. Unfortunately, a big crowd was at the Century Theater, and he couldn't buy tickets. Bart and Anna decided to go to the Dairy Bar and buy ice cream cones instead.

List five common nouns and five proper nouns.

_____

_____

Put a C by nouns that are concrete and A by abstract nouns.

apple	love	rabbit	holiness
bike	intelligence	carrot	bravery

Underline the sentence where the word "train" is used as a noun.

The train left the depot 10 minutes ago. The zookeeper will train the monkey to dance.

Common & Proper Nouns Activities

1. Find out what students know about nouns. Make a chart listing noun facts they offer. Write the definition of a noun on a chart and emphasize that nouns are naming words. Write a few sentences on the board. Ask students to identify and underline the nouns and help them see that nouns occur in all parts of the sentences.

2. Discuss the difference between common and proper nouns and concrete and abstract nouns. Ask the students to give examples of each.

3. Emphasize that a word's part of speech depends on its usage in the sentence. Use examples like the word "name" or "brand." Brand can be a noun as in "The brand of jean I like best is Chic." It can be a verb as in "The cowboys brand the cattle," or an adjective as in "The brand new book is mine."

4. Tell the students that in order to determine if a word is used as a noun in a sentence, they must ask the question, "Does the word name a person, place, or thing?"

5. Use words like name, cage, and fire in various sentences so students can practice determining if a word is used as a noun.

6. Divide a large sheet of paper into two columns labeled Proper Nouns and Common Nouns. Ask the students to name all the nouns they see in the classroom, including names of students and brand name objects for the Proper Noun column.

7. Partner the students and distribute a magazine to each group. The students will be making a noun poster. They should choose a picture for their poster, paste it on a large piece of construction paper and, below it, using a marker, write all the nouns they can find in the picture. For instance, if they choose a picture of an animal, they could list all the animal's body features (nose, mouth, mane,) as well as listing nouns for what they see in the picture's background. Most of the nouns they list will be common nouns, but, if they have chosen a picture of a famous person or place or wish to give names to people or animals in the picture, they will have proper nouns as well. Post the posters.

8. Game: Divide the class into three or four teams. Give each team a word. The team will have one minute to list all the nouns that naturally stem from that one noun. For example: peanut might lead to butter, jar, sandwich, jelly, lunch, breakfast, refrigerator, store, cookies, and nuts. Have the teams exchange lists for correction. If no other part of speech is found, the team is a winner.

9. Review each student handout before assigning.

Student Handout 1 | Common Nouns

Name _____ Date _____

☆ Nouns are names for persons, places, or things. A common noun is the name for any person, place, or thing, like *city, man,* or *fear* and is not capitalized. Nouns can appear anywhere in a sentence. ☆

Look in your desk. Write all the names of objects you see there that are common nouns.

_____

_____

_____.

Finish this list by writing common nouns that begin with the last letter of the preceding noun. It's started for you. Fill up the line with common nouns.

book   kitchen   nose   e _____

Here is a story to make you think.
Can you find and circle 17 common nouns?

George was trying to be quiet as he slipped into his seat at school. He was late and hoped the teacher wouldn't see him. Unfortunately, he tripped over a pencil in the aisle and fell with a loud bang. All the students began to laugh. George started to get up and hit his head on Kim's desk. There are two things he could do; which choice would you make? Circle your choice.

He could get up, look down at the floor, and rush out of the room.
He could get up from the floor, rub his head and say, "I bet I made your day."

In which sentence is the word "tag" used as a noun? Underline it.

Tag is my favorite game. When I play, I try to tag everyone I see.

Student Handout 2 Proper Nouns

Name _____ Date _____

☆ A common noun is the name for any person, place, or thing like city or love. Proper nouns are the names for specific persons, places, or things like *Batman*, *Spain*, or *Mercedes*. ☆

Below is a list of proper nouns. Notice that proper nouns are always CAPITALIZED! Can you name the common noun that describes each one?

Mrs. Jones ___lady___

Cocker Spaniel _____

Manx _____

Levis _____

Denver _____

Boeing 707 ___airplane___

Macintosh _____

Mr. Taylor _____

Reebok _____

Maine _____

The brand names of the food you eat, the clothes you wear, the cars you ride in, the name of your school, city and state where you live, stores where you shop— they are all proper nouns. Use the back of this paper to write a brand name for each of the following categories. (Example: car: Ford)

department store, hospital, street, city, school, church, pharmacy, plumber, jeans, sneakers, dog food, pear, car, grocery store, governor, cat breed, kitchen appliance

BRAND NAMES

The capitals for proper nouns are missing in the following tongue twisters.

Please put capitals where they belong, then say the sentences as fast as you can!

Sister susie sewed shirts for sammy smith while sheila shoveled snow in chicago.

Bathing beauty barbara bought buicks, barbies, and baby ruths in boston.

Lesson 2 Singular & Plural Nouns

Singular & Plural Nouns Teacher Information

Definitions
Singular nouns refer to one person, place, or thing.
Plural nouns refer to more than one person, place, or thing.
Regular nouns are nouns that follow specific rules to change from singular to plural.
Irregular nouns are nouns that do not follow any rules to become plural.

Changing Singular Nouns to Plural Nouns

Regular Nouns

1. Most of the time you make nouns plural by simply adding *s* to the singular form.

    hand   hands   fear   fears   game   games

2. Plurals of nouns that end with *y* are made by changing the *y* to *ie* and adding *s*

    Candy   candies   cherry   cherries   baby   babies

3. Nouns that end with a *y* preceded by a vowel are made plural by adding s.

    Monday   Mondays   monkey   monkeys   buoy   buoys

4. It is the same for words ending in an *o* preceded by another vowel; just add *s*.

    radio   radios   patio   patios   stereo   stereos

5. Most nouns ending with only one vowel, an *o*, are made plural by adding *es* but some need only an *s* to make them plural. Musical terms, for instance, always take only an *s* (soprano, sopranos; piano, pianos). Other examples are autos, memos, Pimientos. Check the dictionary.

    potato   potatoes   tomato   tomatoes   zero   zeroes   echo   echoes

6. For words that end in *f* or *fe,* change the *f* to *v* and add *es* or *s* or just add an *s* to the word as it is. Again, it's best to check the dictionary.

    knife   knives   hoof   hooves   leaf   leaves   dwarf   dwarfs

7. Words ending in *s, ss, z, sh, ch*, and *x* get *es* to make the plural.

    gas   gases   kiss   kisses   buzz   buzzes   box   boxes

Irregular Nouns

1. Irregular nouns do not follow any rule to form their plurals. They form them in many different ways.

    child   children   mouse   mice   man   men   goose   geese

2. Some irregular nouns remain the same.

    Deer and sheep are the same in the singular and the plural forms.

✓ Singular and Plural Nouns Pre and Post Test

Write the plural for each of the following words:

pencil _____   baby _____

Tuesday _____   dwarf _____

radio_____   piano _____

tomato_____   miss _____

roof _____   pass_____

fox_____   mix _____

child_____   goose _____

deer _____   house _____

Tell whether the words below are regular or irregular nouns.

cow _____   mouse _____   sheep _____

potato _____   leaf _____   foot _____

Singular & Plural Nouns Activities

1. Post the rules for making plurals, one rule to a piece of paper, around the room, just above students' eye-level, if possible.

2. Explain the rules to the students, finding examples for each rule in the classroom. Discuss exceptions and the need for dictionary skills. This may be a good time to teach or review how to use a dictionary.

3. Divide the class into groups of eight. Give each student in the group an index card on which is written a word that exemplifies one of the rules for changing singular nouns to plural. Ask the students to stand by the posted rule that the word on their card illustrates. *Example: A student who has the word leaf would stand under the rule, "In words that end with f, change the f to v and add es."* When they are all in place, ask each student to read the rule that applies to the word she is holding. Continue until all students have had a chance to find a rule.

4. Divide the class into eight small groups and assign a rule to each group. Ask each group to write the rule on a piece of construction paper and draw pictures of words that illustrate the rule.

5. Review the handout with the students before assigning.

Student Handout 3 | Singular & Plural Regular Nouns

Name _____ Date _____

⭐ Singular nouns refer to one person, place, or thing.
Plural nouns refer to more than one person, place, or thing.

Rewrite the words below as plurals.   **+S**

Add an s to most nouns to make them plural.

book_____   shoe_____   movie_____   monkey_____

In words that end in a y with no other vowel, change the y to ie and then add an s.

hanky_____   piggy_____   mommy_____

Y>IE+S

When a word ends in o, io, or eo, add es or s. Check the dictionary to make sure.

potato_____   tomato_____   stereo_____   radio_____

es or s

Add an s to musical terms that end in o

piano_____   soprano_____   banjo_____

+S

If a word ends in f or fe, add an s or change the f to v and add es or s.

Check the dictionary!

roof_____   leaf_____   knife_____   dwarf_____

es or s

Words ending in s, ss, ch, sh, z, and x need an es to make them plural. This one is easy because you can hear the es you add to the words to make them plural.

box_____   kiss_____   witch_____   wish_____

+es

> Challenge: On the back of this paper, write at least five sentences using as many plural nouns as you can. Use nouns that are examples of all the rules above. Underline the plural nouns in your sentences.
>
> Example: The little *monkeys* climbed the *trees* that were in their *cages.*

Student Handout 4 | Singular & Plural Irregular Nouns

Name _____ Date _____

There are some nouns that don't follow any rules to become plural nouns. They are called irregular nouns.

child children   foot feet   woman women
goose geese   tooth teeth   man men   mouse mice

Some nouns even stay the same whether they are singular or plural.

sheep   deer   moose

Then there are some nouns that can change or stay the same.
Fish can be *fish* or *fishes* in the plural form.

On the back of this paper, draw a picture of yourself. Then label each item of clothing and body part that's visible, writing both the singular and plural forms of the noun.

Fill in the words of this rhyme using plurals.

The plural of fish can be _____ or _____,

But the plural of wish will always be _____.

_____ is the plural of a cute little mouse,

But we always say _____ for the plural of house.

If _____ is the plural for the word tooth,

Then why is _____ the plural of booth?

I know we say _____ for the plural of moose,

But then we say _____ for the plural of goose.

One child turns into a crowd of _____,

And the plural for woman becomes many _____.

Lesson 3 Possessive Nouns

Possessive Nouns Teacher Information

Possessive nouns indicate ownership.

Singular Possessive
To make a singular noun possessive add apostrophe *s* ('s) to all nouns, common or proper, even those that end with the letter s.

boy the boy's pet   Mr. Brown Mr. Brown's hat   lass the lass's dress

Plural Possessive
For plural nouns that end in *s* or *es,* just add an apostrophe.

cars the cars' horns   ladies the ladies' hats

Irregular Possessives
Add *'s* to irregular nouns to make the possessive form.

men men's   women women's
children children's   sheep sheep's

One or More Owners
If one item is owned by two people, only the second name gets the apostrophe s.

Jane and Sam's car was in an accident. (only one car)

If two people each own separate items, both names get apostrophe *s*.

Jane's and Sam's cars were wrecked. (two cars)

✓ Possessive Nouns Pre and Post Test

Fill in the correct possessive nouns.

The _____ hat was red. (girl) The _____ hats were blue. (girls)

The beautiful _____ eyes were wet with tears. (lass)

The _____ cars were wrecked in the accident. (men)

_____ car was covered with snow. (Bob and Pedro)

_____ dresses were identical. (Juana and Estelle)

Write two sentences telling about something you or a friend owns.

_____

_____

_____

Lesson 3 Possessive Nouns

Possessive Nouns Activities

1. Explain how possessives are made.

2. Ask students to make a list of people in their family or friends along with one of their possessions. Example: *Mom's car; Dad's golf club; neighbor's yard.*

3. Choose two or three students at a time and give them something like an eraser or pencil. Ask the class to tell how they would indicate that all two or three own the one object. Example: *Mary, Todd, and Sue's eraser.* Now give two students each an eraser and ask how that would be expressed: *Mary's and Todd's erasers.*

4. Write a list of nouns on the board, some singular, some plural, and some irregular; ask students to change them to the possessive form.

5. Dictate the following short paragraph. Correct together. *The storm was finally over, but the worst was yet to come. Marco's and Nick's boats were nowhere to be seen. The ocean's waves broke over the shore, still rough after the night's storm. The Coast Guard's ship started out to look for the boys' boats when everyone saw a welcome sight. Two boats came over the horizon, and the sun's rays suddenly broke out, as did everyone's shouts of welcome to Marco and Nick.*

6. Review the student handout before assigning.

Student Handout 5 | Possessive Nouns

Name _____ Date _____

Change singular regular nouns and irregular nouns, both singular and plural, to the possessive form by adding an *apostrophe* and an s. Add an 's to the first word in each pair of words. Then write a sentence using one of the possessive nouns.

children___ pails   boy___ swim fins   foot___ toes   bus___ old seats

_____

Add only an *apostrophe* to the plurals of regular nouns ending in an s. Add the apostrophe to the first word in each pair and then write a sentence using one of the possessive nouns.

girls__ bikes   schools__ classrooms   hands__ fingers   shoes__ heels

_____

When two or more people own one thing, the *apostrophe* s goes after the last person's name. Rewrite the nouns as possessive nouns with the correct *apostrophe* s.

Mario and Tom caught a big fish. _____fish

Mr. and Mrs. Schmidt have a boat. _____boat

If two people each own something, both names get an *apostrophe* s. Rewrite the nouns as possessive nouns.

Jennie and Mimi both have birthday parties. _____ parties

Carlo and Max have surfboards. _____ surfboards

Rewrite using possessive nouns.
Example: The party of Michelle: Michelle's party.

the tents of Giovanni and Peter: _____

the basketballs of the boy and girl: _____

the car of Mr. and Mrs. Perez: _____

13

Review, Lessons One through Three

Name _____ Date _____

Following is a listing of both common and proper nouns. Rewrite the nouns using capital letters where needed. Put a *C* above the common nouns and a *P* above the proper nouns.

cat_____ chevrolet_____ nike_____

amusement park_____ sea world_____

amanda_____ dairy queen_____ computer_____

There are many ways to make the plurals of nouns. Rewrite the following nouns in their plural form.

tree	_____	age	_____	kiss	_____	woman	_____
fly	_____	turkey	_____	calf	_____	child	_____
box	_____	enemy	_____	tooth	_____	wife	_____
piano	_____	house	_____	monkey	_____	hero	_____

Here are some of the rules for changing singular nouns to their plural form.

Complete each rule and change the singular noun that follows the rule to its plural form.

1. The plural of most nouns is formed by adding ____ to the singular. bagel _____

2. The plural of most nouns ending in *ch, s, sh, x,* and *z* is formed by adding ____ to the singular. brush
_____

3. Nouns ending in a consonant and *y* change ____ to ____ and add ____. study _____

4. Nouns ending in a vowel and *y* add ____. valley _____

5. Many nouns that end in *f* or *fe* change the ____ to ____ and add ____ or ____.
   wolf _____ wife _____

6. Most nouns ending in *o* add ____ to make the plural. piano _____

7. Some nouns ending in *o* add ____. tomato _____

8. Irregular nouns don't follow any _____ to change from singular to plural.
   goose _____ moose _____ mouse _____

Nouns form the possessive case in a few different ways. Write the plural of each word below and then write the possessive case for both the singular and the plural words.

Singular	Possessive	Plural	Possessive
boy	boy's	boys	boys'
child			
monkey			
lass			
secretary			
man			
woman			
lady			

Write four sentences about some things that the members of your family and your friends own. Use the possessive form of the nouns.

Example: My family's car is brand new.

Lesson 4 Personal Pronouns

Personal Pronouns Teacher Information

Pronouns take the place of nouns in sentences and are used the same way nouns are used.

Juana carried the *basket* to her Mama. Juana carried *it* to her Mama.
              noun   pronoun

Maria put fruit in the basket. *She* put fruit in the basket.
 noun   pronoun

Jacob went on a trip with his *friends*. Jacob went on a trip with *them*.
                     noun   pronoun

Personal Pronouns

I, we, my, mine, our, ours, me, us, you, your, yours, yourself, yourselves, he, she, it, they, his, her, hers, its, their, theirs, him, them, himself, herself, itself, themselves

Some adjectives can also serve as pronouns: *this, that, these, and those.*

This stinks! *That* was a hard test.

Uses of Personal Pronouns

Personal pronouns can be used in many ways in a sentence.

They can serve as the subject of the sentence: *She* wanted to pass the test.

They can follow a preposition like *to, in, with, near*: Josie went with *them*.

As intensive personal pronouns, they serve to emphasize meaning: "I *myself* made all the flowers for the dance."

Agreement with Noun

If a pronoun follows a noun in a sentence, it must agree with the word or words it refers to, its antecedent, in number and person. To decide what pronoun to use, first determine what the subject of the sentence is (who or what the sentence is about) and whether it is singular or plural, masculine or feminine.

Anna went home because *she* was sick. (Anna is the subject. It is singular and feminine.)

Then *John, Terri, and Sam* got sick, and *they* had to go home.

(The subject of this sentence is John, Terri, and Sam. Because there is more than one person, we need a plural pronoun.)

The *teacher,* Mr. Klein, felt sick too, but *he* had to stay in school.

(Teacher is the subject. His name tells us we need a masculine pronoun.)

Using the Pronouns Me and I

I is a pronoun that will always be used as a subject or a predicate nominative in a sentence.

Subject: *I* will go. Jeffrey and *I* will go. Jeffrey, Josh, and *I* will go.

Predicate Nominative: It is *I* who will go to the fair.

Me is used as the object of prepositions like *with, to,* and *near,* and as a direct object.

Object of preposition: They will go with *me*. They live near *me* and Tom.

Direct object: He hit *me*. When her parents went on vacation, Anna missed *them*.
Note: See Lesson Fourteen for more information about predicate nominatives and objects.
A good way to remember the placement of *I* and *me* is that most of the time *I* will be used toward the beginning of a sentence in the subject and *me* in the latter part of a sentence.

✓ Personal Pronouns Pre and Post Test

Follow the instructions.

Tell what a pronoun is. _____

List several personal pronouns. _____

_____

Use four of those pronouns in sentences to show how a personal pronoun can be used as the subject of the sentence and after a preposition like with, in, or to.

_____

_____

_____

_____

What are two intensive personal pronouns that can add emphasis to a sentence?

_____   _____

Underline the subject of each sentence. Then fill in the correct pronoun.

Mario didn't think _____ could swim faster than the other swimmers.

His friends said _____ would cheer him on.

Max, Celeste, and Tina cheered very loudly, and _____ helped Mario finish first.

Fill in I or me in the following sentences.

Jorge and _____ will go to the show. Mom gave the tickets to _____ and Jorge.

Personal Pronouns Activities

1. Discuss what personal pronouns are and how they function. List the personal pronouns on the board or a chart. Point to or name people and objects in the room and ask students to name the correct pronoun for each.

2. Give examples of the different ways personal pronouns can be used in sentences.

3. Discuss how the words *I* and *me* should be used in a sentence.

4. Give some examples of both the proper way to use the words *I* and *me* and the improper way to use them. Ask students to give sentences using *I* as the subject and predicate nominative and *me* as the object of a preposition and as a direct object.

5. Dictate several sentences that are examples of the different uses of personal pronouns. Correct together by writing the sentences on the board. Examples: *Mary made the cookies herself; she baked and put decorations on them. Her parents said they had never tasted such good cookies.*

6. Discuss the sentences the students wrote in step three above. Point out how the pronoun used in each sentence agrees with the noun.

7. Tell the students they are going to write a class story; write it on a chart as they dictate it. The story will have as many sentences as there are students in the room plus the starter sentence, which the teacher will supply, and at least every other sentence must include a personal pronoun. The students must add on to the beginning sentence to create a story that makes sense. Use the beginning sentence below or make up one that is relevant to the classroom. Beginning sentence: *Barry was sure he had locked the snake's cage.*

8. Review the student handout before assigning.

Student Handout 6   Personal Pronouns

Name _____ Date _____

Personal pronouns take the place of nouns in a sentence and can be used in the same ways that nouns are used. Here are some personal pronouns.

I, we, you, he, she, it, they, me, us, you, him, her, them, my, mine, our, ours, your, yours, his, hers, its, their, theirs, whose, myself, yourself, yourselves, himself, herself, itself

Write three sentences using personal pronouns in different ways.

As the subject of a sentence:

_____.

After a preposition like *in, with, to,* or *near*:

_____.

To show emphasis:

_____.

When a pronoun refers to a noun or nouns that come before it, it must agree with the noun or nouns in number and person. Here are some examples. *Anna* can't come because *she* is grounded. The *children* were so quiet *they* surprised me. Underline the subject in each sentence. Fill in the blanks with the pronoun that agrees with the subject. Then put the words on the lines after the sentences.

John is lazy and _____ never does his homework.   __ __

The teachers say _____do not give too much homework.   __ __ __ __

Pat and John will do _____homework together.   __ __ __ __ __

Look at the letters you wrote on the side of the sentences. There should be one pronoun that you can read diagonally. Write a sentence using that pronoun correctly.

_____.

Lesson 5 Indefinite Pronouns

Indefinite Pronouns Teacher Information

Indefinite Pronouns refer to people or things in general—that's why they are called indefinite! Some indefinite pronouns are *all, any, anybody, anyone, each, either, everybody, everyone, few, many, most, other, some, another, both, either, neither, nobody, none, no one, several, somebody, someone.*

Referring to Large Groups: Indefinite pronouns make it easier in many situations to address or refer to a large group of people or objects.
Did anyone see the thief? Does everybody want to ski? Most of the chairs are broken.

Clarifying Instructions: They also help in clarifying instructions.
Answer all questions. Assemble each part in the order listed. Choose either essay.

Number Sense: Some indefinite pronouns give an idea about the number of people, places, or things.
Several people saw the thief. No one wants to ski. None of the questions make sense.

Verb Agreement with Indefinite Pronouns
When indefinite pronouns are the subject of a sentence, they can be singular or plural and need to take either a singular or plural form of verb. A few pronouns can be either singular or plural depending on how they are used in the sentence.

Singular
The words *another, anyone, anybody, anything, each, either, everyone, everybody, everything, neither, no one, nobody, nothing, one, someone,* and *somebody* are singular pronouns and take a singular verb form.
Somebody has left a backpack on the bench. *No one goes shopping* without any money.

Plural Indefinite Pronouns
Both, many, and *several* are plural pronouns that take the plural verb form.
Both boys *want* new bikes. *Many* teachers *are* nice. *Several* girls *go* swimming here.

Indefinite Pronouns That Can Be Singular or Plural
Some indefinite pronouns, like *none* or *some*, can be either singular or plural.
Some of the books *were* heavy. *Some* refers to a plural noun so it is plural.
Some of the milk *was* sour. *Some* refers to a singular noun so it is singular.

✓ Indefinite Pronouns Pre and Post Test
Follow the instructions.

Write five sentences using the indefinite pronouns all, everybody, nobody, most, and none.

_____

_____

_____

_____

Lesson 5 Indefinite Pronouns

Fill in an indefinite pronoun in the following sentences.

Does _____ want some ice cream?

_____ of the class wanted to go on a field trip to the zoo.

_____ moved the snake from its cage.

_____ is looking for the snake.

Underline the indefinite pronoun that is the subject of each sentence. Then choose the correct verb for the sentences.

None of the sandwiches _____ spoiled. (was, were)

Both girls _____ new dresses. (want, wants)

No one _____ done the homework. (have, has)

Indefinite Pronouns Activities

1. Discuss when it would be appropriate to use indefinite pronouns: when referring to people, places, or things in general rather than specifically. For instance, suppose a person wanted to serve pie to a large gathering. Instead of naming everyone in the room and asking them individually if they want pie, it's much easier to ask of the room in general, "Does anyone want some pie?"

2. Ask students to think of a question they might want to ask the class using an indefinite pronoun. Students must answer also using an indefinite pronoun. Here's an example. Question: *Does anybody want to go to detention this afternoon?*

   Answer: *Nobody wants to go to detention this afternoon.*

3. Dictate a few sentences to the students omitting the indefinite pronoun. Ask them to insert one that would make sense. Example: I want to take _____ pastries. Share sentences to see how many different indefinite pronouns the students used.

4. Explain that some indefinite pronouns are singular, some are plural, and some can be either. Practice using pronouns that use singular and plural verbs. Write various verbs on index cards and distribute several to each student. Read aloud a sentence that includes an indefinite pronoun omitting the verb. Ask students to hold up index cards that would be grammatically correct to use in the sentence. Example: *Everyone _____ a bike.* Students would hold up a singular verb like sees, has, or wants. Say the sentence aloud with the suggested verbs and discuss why they are good choices. For the sentence, *"Many children _____ basketball,"* students would hold up a plural verb.

5. Review the student handout before assigning.

Student Handout 7 | Indefinite Pronouns

Name _____ Date _____

Indefinite pronouns refer to people or things in general; that's why they are called indefinite! *Another, anyone, anybody, anything, each, either, everyone, everybody, everything, neither, no one, nobody, nothing, one, someone,* and *somebody* are indefinite pronouns that take a singular verb. *Everyone is here.*

Both, many, and *several* are indefinite pronouns that take a plural verb. *Both girls are here.*

Some indefinite pronouns, like *none* or *some,* can be either singular or plural.

Write five indefinite pronouns that can make sense in each sentence.

a) _____ wants to go to the party.

_____   _____   _____   _____   _____

b) _____ admitted to stealing the presents.

_____   _____   _____   _____   _____

c) Then the girls found _____ of the presents.

_____   _____   _____   _____   _____

Underline the correct pronoun in the following sentences.

Everyone can come to the party if (his/her   their) parents say it's okay.

Each student said (they   he/she) would be able to attend.

Someone forgot to ask (their   his/her) parents for permission.

When I asked the partygoers, several said (they   he/she) had a good time.

Write three sentences using these indefinite pronouns: everybody, both, none.

_____

_____

_____

_____

Lesson 6 Possessive Pronouns

Possessive Pronouns Teacher Information

Possessive Pronouns
Possessive pronouns show ownership. Possessive pronouns *never* have an apostrophe.
They are *its; whose; her, hers; his; my, mine; our, ours; their, theirs; your, yours.*

Contractions versus Possessive Pronouns
(See Lesson 19 for more on contractions.)
Very often, people confuse contractions with possessive pronouns. Examples:

its = possessive pronoun   it's = it is, contraction
The dog ate *its* supper.   *It's* good for him.
their = possessive pronoun   they're = they are, contraction
This is *their* dog.   *They're* taking a ride on a camel.

Who or Whom?
In modern usage, it is proper to use *who* most of the time unless it comes after a preposition. *To whom shall I give the book? For whom are you calling?*

✓ Possessive Pronouns Pre and Post Test

Fill in the correct pronoun or contraction.

it's or its   My boss thinks _____ time to work. The lion escaped from _____ cage.

you're or your   Is this _____ snake? I think _____ a good friend.

Whose or Who's   _____ mother is that? _____ your mother?

Fill in who or whom.

To _____ should I address this letter?

_____ is going to the hockey game with me?

I don't know _____ gave me this gift.

Write five sentences using the possessive form of it, their, you, our, who.

_____

_____

_____

_____

_____

_____

_____

Possessive Pronouns Activities

1. Review how to make possessive pronouns emphasizing the fact that no apostrophes are needed. Dictate several sentences using possessive pronouns. Discuss each sentence after it is written before going on to the next sentence. Examples: *The dog buried its bone. The campers put out their fire.*

2. Show pictures from magazines or books that demonstrate possession. For instance, show a picture of a baby holding a teddy bear. Ask students to describe the picture by writing a sentence that includes a possessive pronoun. *The baby is holding her teddy bear.*

3. Distribute old magazines. Have students divide a piece of drawing paper into four boxes. In each box, students should put a picture from the magazine and a sentence using a possessive pronoun. Post the pictures when they are done.

4. Discuss the difference between possessive pronouns and contractions. Post the examples listed in the teacher information section. (*it's* and *its*, for example) Use several sentences to demonstrate how to use both forms. Examples: *Who's in the house? Whose house is this?* Ask students to write either a contraction or a possessive pronoun on the board and give a sentence using the word. The other students can decide if the word is used correctly.

5. Review the student handout before assigning.

Student Handout 8 | Possessive Pronouns

Name _____ Date _____

⭐ Possessive pronouns show ownership and never have an apostrophe. Possessive pronouns are: *its; whose; her, hers; his; my, mine; our, ours; their, theirs; your, yours.* ⭐

Finish the sentences using the possessive pronouns indicated for each one.

The big bear _____ (its)

The girl didn't know _____ (whose)

Jack and Jill _____ (their)

I see some _____ (your)

If you see an *apostrophe s* or an *apostrophe re* after a pronoun, it is a contraction, and you have to tack on the word *is* or the word *are*.

Possessive Pronouns	Contractions
its	*it's (it is)*
whose	*who's (who is)*
their	*they're (they are)*
your	*you're (you are)*

Fill in the following sentences with either a possessive pronoun or a contraction.

_____ picture is _____ favorite? (Whose or Who's / your or you're)

The dog was licking _____ paw.   (it's or its)

My brother and sister pass down _____ clothes to me. (they're or their)

_____ so nice to give me _____ lunch. (You're or Your/ you're or your)

Challenge: On the back of this paper, draw three pictures to illustrate three different possessive pronouns. Write a sentence that includes the pronouns for each picture.

CHALLENGE

Lesson 7 Adjectives

Adjectives Teacher Information

Adjectives give information and answer certain questions about nouns and pronouns: Which one? What kind? Whose? How many? Most come before the noun they modify.

Descriptive adjectives do just what their name says they do; they describe nouns and pronouns. The *tall* man, the *ferocious* lion, and the *green* apple are examples. Descriptive adjectives can also be used to make comparisons like *sweet, sweeter,* and *sweetest* or *good, better, best.*

Demonstrative pronouns are used as adjectives. They indicate certain people or objects and tell something about their distance from you—*that, these, this, those, which,* and *what. That girl* indicates a particular girl and shows she is not close to the speaker. *This boy* indicates a certain boy and shows that he is close to the speaker. Four of these words can be used by themselves as pronouns—*this, that, these,* and *those. This* is mine. *That* is yours. *These* belong to my mom. *Those* are your pet's.

Limiting adjectives identify (*a* ball, *the* apple) or indicate an amount or number (*some* students, *several* desks). *A, an, each, every, many, most, several,* and *some* are examples of limiting adjective.

A **predicate adjective** follows a linking verb like feel, look, seem, smell, taste. The verb links the noun with the adjective. Examples: The girl feels *hot.* She looks *pale.*

Compound adjectives use a hyphen as in *brown-haired* boy or *three-toed* sloth. You do not use hyphens if the adjectives come after the noun. *The sloth was three toed.*

Articles: *A, an,* and *the* are adjectives that are called articles: *the girl, a car, an apple.*

✓ Adjectives Pre and Post Test

Circle the adjectives.

The rotten banana in the ceramic bowl is turning black.

Those horses in the corral are race horses.

The teacher was happy that her brilliant students aced the difficult test.

The blue-eyed girl wore a long frilly dress that matched her eyes.

Fill in appropriate adjectives.

I really like the _____scarf. We play _____ kinds of games. Tim wants to ride _____ horse over there. After she fell, the little girl looked _____.

Draw a line from the kind of adjective to its example.

Descriptive adjective	I think that girl will win the spelling bee.
Demonstrative Adjective	She rode the fiery horse without falling.
Predicate Adjective	It was a battery-powered car.
Limiting Adjective	She felt sad.
Compound Adjective	I had several candies in my mouth.

25

Adjectives Activities

1. Discuss the various kinds of adjectives and their usage. Mention that *a, an*, and *the* are also called articles.

2. Use adjectives to describe objects in the classroom.

3. Play a few different kinds of music and ask students to write a list of adjectives that describe each type of music.

4. Put an object into a brown paper bag. Ask the students to feel the object through the bag, write adjectives to describe what they feel, then guess what is in the bag.

5. Write lists of demonstrative, limiting, and predicate adjectives on a chart. Make up a round robin story with the teacher providing the first sentence in the story and each student in turn adding a sentence. Ask students to use as many kinds of adjectives as they can. Example for a starting sentence: *That old* man wants to get into *the silver* rocket ship. Write the story on chart paper as it is dictated. When the story is done, ask students to underline each type of adjective with a different color marker.

6. Explain that we use a compound adjective when the adjective comes before the noun it modifies but not when it comes after the noun. Give examples. Examples: The city has a *well-run* program for after school care. The city's after school care program is *well run.*

7. Give the students a few compound adjectives and ask them to write two sentences, one using the compound adjective and one where it is not necessary to use it.

8. Examples: *Blue-eyed, school-owned, battery-operated.*

9. Review the student handout before assigning.

Student Handout 9 | Adjectives One

Name _____ Date _____

Descriptive adjectives describe a noun or pronoun.

(speech bubble: Descriptive adjectives)

The following story is very boring. That's because it needs more adjectives. Help the reader to picture the story by adding some adjectives.

The _____ fisherman stood on the dock and threw his line into the _____ water. After only a minute, he felt a _____ tug on his line. He pulled and pulled and finally fell backwards onto the _____ dock as he pulled a _____ mermaid from the water. The mermaid began to cry, _____ tears falling down her _____ face. "I will die if I don't get back into the water now," she wailed. Her _____ screams touched the fisherman's _____ heart, and he slipped the _____ mermaid back into the water.

Demonstrative adjectives indicate certain people or objects and tell something about their distance from you. (*that, these, this, those, which,* and *what*)

(speech bubble: Demonstrative adjectives)

Put a demonstrative adjective in each of the following sentences.

I like _____ horse over there. _____ horse is stepping on my foot.

_____ is the horse you like best? On _____ planet are there horses?

I like _____ horse over in the field. _____ horse is yours?

Have you read _____ horse books here on the table?

Now read the *third* word in each of the above sentences to solve this riddle.

Why is Mars like a book? _____

On the back of this paper write three sentences using as many of the demonstrative adjectives as possible.

Example: *That* boy gave me *these* books to put on *this* table.

Student Handout 10 | Adjectives Two

Name _____ Date _____

Limiting adjectives identify (*a* ball, *the* apple) or indicate an amount or number (*some* students, *several* desks). *A, an, each, every, many, most, several,* and *some* are limiting adjectives.
A, the, and *an* are also called articles.

Write all the limiting adjectives or articles that could be used in these sentences.

_____ girls like to play soccer. _____ _____ _____

I want to try _____ apple. _____ _____

We are going to visit _____ cities. _____ _____ _____

A predicate adjective follows a linking verb like *feel, look, seem, smell, taste.* The verb links the noun with the adjective. The man *feels* dizzy. He *looks* sick.

Write three sentences using some of the linking verbs above with predicate adjectives.

_____

_____

_____

Compound adjectives use a hyphen as in *black-haired* lady or *sure-footed* runner.

Circle all the compound adjectives that tell about you and write three sentences using some of those adjectives.

sure-footed	peace-keeping	know-it-all	bare-footed	well-shod
curly-haired	straight-haired	grass-covered	sweet-loving	blue-eyed
green-eyed	brown-eyed	left-handed	right-handed	short-haired long-haired

_____

_____

_____

Name _____ Date _____

In sentences two through four below, replace the subject of the sentence with a pronoun.

1. Arthur has a pet rabbit that was a birthday gift.
2. Arthur feeds the rabbit and cleans its cage with his mother's help.
3. His mother washes the rabbit's dish after Arthur empties it.
4. Arthur and his mother really love the sweet pet.

Draw a line to the pronoun that best completes each sentence.

Everyone must bring _____ money for the zoo.   their

The monkeys escaped from _____ cage.   his or her

Raul and I lost _____ lunches at the park.   their

I _____ had packed those lunches   her

Any girl who wants to go must have permission from _____ parents.   them

Several students forgot _____ permission slips.   myself

The teachers wanted to keep the students near _____.   our

Fill in the either *I* or *me* in the sentences below.

Juana and _____ are going to the movies.

Some other friends will meet _____ and Juana at the theater.

My mom gave us plenty of money, so Juana and _____ can buy some treats.

The movie is one that Juana and _____ have wanted to see for a long time.

Some adjectives act as pronouns. Fill in the word that best completes the sentences.

that   this   these   those

I like _____.   (shoes in the store across the street)

_____ is my favorite. (holding a book)

_____ are the perfect earrings. (trying on earrings)

Hand me _____, please. (pointing to a dish)

Some pronouns can be either singular or plural. Fill in either *were* or *was* in the sentences.

Some of the trucks _____ going too fast.

Most of the ice cream _____ melted.

Most of the girls _____ at the meeting.

Some of the milk _____ spoiled.

Possessive pronouns are often confused with contractions. Choose the words that fit best in the sentences below: *it's, its; your, you're; their, they're.*

_____ time to go. Where is _____ coat? _____ waiting for us. Oh, no!

The car lost _____ muffler. Now _____ going to have to find another car.

Maybe the neighbors will lend you _____ car.

Use descriptive adjectives to complete the sentences.

The _____ lion paced in its cage and gave a _____ roar that frightened

some _____ children standing near.

Choose the demonstrative adjective that best fits each sentence: *which, that, this.*

I like _____ bike over there in the window. _____ bike that I am riding

is not half as nice. _____ bike do you like best?

Choose among the limiting adjectives *a, an, each, every, many, most, several,* and *some* **to tell the following story your way.**

Our class voted on _____ trip for class day. _____ of the class wanted

to go to a theme park. _____ voted for lunch in a restaurant and a movie.

The teacher counted _____ vote and told us the result.

Answer this question. What was the result of the vote based on the adjectives you used

in the sentences? We ended up going to _____.

Complete the following sentences with a predicate adjective.

Laura feels _____ because she can't go to the state fair.

The bed looks like it's too _____ for me. This test seems very _____.

Combine the words below to make compound adjectives.

sure	footed	_____	right	handed	_____
blue	eyed	_____	long	haired	_____
grass	covered	_____	bare	footed	_____

Write two sentences using two of the compound adjectives above.

_____

_____

Lesson 8 Verbs

Verbs Teacher Information

Verbs describe action or a state of being. Every complete sentence must have a verb.
Action: The children *ran* through the tall grass.
State of being: The children *are* happy.

Regular and Irregular Verbs
A regular verb is defined as one that follows the same pattern when moving from one tense to another. Example: A regular verb adds *ed* to its base to make the past tense.

stroll   strolled   pass   passed   want   wanted

An irregular verb is one that does not follow a pattern when moving from one tense to another. Example: The past tense of *run* is *ran*.   The past tense of *send* is *sent*.

Linking Verbs
A verb is called a linking verb if it describes a state of being and links a predicate adjective to a noun.

The girls *are* polite. *Are* links and shows the connection between girls and polite.

Some linking verbs are *feel, taste, sound, smell, look, seem,* and any form of the verb *be*.

Transitive and Intransitive Verbs
Transitive verbs must have an object (some thing) to complete their meaning.

Beth *hung* the picture on her bedroom wall. The verb *hung* is followed by an object, a picture.

Intransitive verbs do not have an object to complete their meaning.

She *waited* for hours. The dog *jumped* very high.

Linking verbs are intransitive because they are not followed by an object.
Louisa *was* happy when her friends visited her.

Helping or Auxiliary Verbs
Helping verbs come right before and help other present, past, and future tense verbs do their job. The most commonly used helping verbs are *am, is, are, was, were, be, been, do, does, did, have, has, had, will, shall, can, may, must, would, should,* and *could*.
(See Lesson 11 for more on auxiliary verbs.)

She *is* eating her dinner. We *were* going to the opera. Raul *will* try to hit a homer.

✓ Verbs Pre and Post Test

Circle the verb in the following sentences. Then circle what kind of a verb it is.

The girls ran in the race.	Regular	Irregular
Jennie felt happy to come in first.	Transitive	Linking
The track coach gave her a medal.	Transitive	Intransitive
Her teammates jumped up and down for joy.	Regular	Irregular
Her parents clapped very loudly.	Transitive	Intransitive
They were proud of their daughter.	Regular	Linking

Add a helping verb to these sentences:

The boys' relay team _____ won its race too.

You _____ run your very best.

I _____ know what game you want to play.

Verbs Activities

1. Explain that verbs are words that describe action or a state of being. Give examples and ask the students to name some verbs too. The babies *cried*. They *were* unhappy.

2. Look through any text and ask students to read sentences identifying the verbs as they read.

3. Explain that there are several different kinds of verbs and name them: regular, irregular, transitive, intransitive, helping, and linking. Define these types of verbs one at a time and find examples of them in any text or story book.

4. Dictate several sentences containing examples of the verbs named above. Ask students to underline the verb and identify what kind of verb it is.

5. Show pictures from a magazine and ask students to write or say sentences that tell what is happening in the picture, including the feelings of anyone in the picture. Ask them to identify the kind of verb they used in the sentence.

6. Bingo. Distribute large-squared graph paper to the students and ask them to make a Bingo card by putting a verb in each of 25 boxes. Tell the students they will be playing Bingo using all the different kinds of verbs. As the teacher calls out the various kinds of verbs, the students put a marker on one verb that is called by that name. Example: Call out "regular," and the students pick one verb on their Bingo card that could be classified as a regular verb.

7. Check the Bingo cards of the winners as a class for a review of the terms.

8. Review the handout before assigning.

Student Handout 11 | Verbs

Name _____ Date _____

> **Verbs describe action or a state of being.** Circle the verbs in the sentences.
>
> Chuck ran a good race and won a gold medal.
>
> Sandy finished in second place and earned a red ribbon.
>
> Raul felt happy for his friends.

Regular verbs make the past tense by adding ed to the base word.

Irregular verbs don't have any rule for making the past tense.

Write the past tense of these verbs and tell whether they are regular or irregular.

like _____ _____   see _____ _____

limp _____ _____   run _____ _____

Linking verbs are verbs that describe a state of being and link an adjective to a noun. Example: Perry was happy. Write three sentences using a linking verb.

_____

_____

_____

Transitive verbs must have an object to complete their meaning.

I *have* a cat.

Intransitive verbs do not have an object to complete their meaning.

I *ran* quickly.

Write T or I to show whether the verb is transitive or intransitive.

Mel has a book. _____   Juanita loves to dance _____

Mario won a prize. _____   Marc wanted to fly. _____

Lisette made her bed. _____   James skis very fast. _____

Helping verbs like *have*, *had*, *must*, and *am* work with other verbs.

Fill in a helping verb. I _____ eaten my breakfast.

Dad _____ gone for a walk before breakfast.

Mom said I _____ do my homework.

I _____ doing it now.

Lesson 9 Forming Verb Tenses

Forming Verb Tenses Teacher Information

Regular verbs follow a set rule for forming the **past and future tenses** of the verb. Here are the present, past, and future tenses of some regular verbs.

Present	**Past (add *d* or *ed*)**	**Future**
walk	*walked*	*will walk*
bike	*biked*	*will bike*

Irregular verbs follow no set rule for forming the past tense of the verb but make the future tense the same way that regular verbs do.

Present	**Past**	**Future**
ring	*rang*	*will ring*
run	*ran*	*will run*
break	*broke*	*will break*

Progressive Verbs   The progressive form of a verb ends in *ing* and shows that the action is ongoing, not completed. Progressive verbs use a helping verb.
The bells have been *ringing* for an hour. Dad is *napping*. The cooks are *baking*.

Doubling the Final Consonant   If a verb has a short vowel, the ending consonant must be doubled before adding *ing* or *ed: run, running; fan, fanning, fanned; win, winning; nap, napping, napped.*

Dropping the Final E   Verbs that end in *e* drop the *e* before adding *ing: make, making.*

✓ Forming Verb Tenses Pre and Post Test

Write the past and future tenses of the following verbs. Which verbs are regular and which are irregular?

jump   _____   _____   regular or irregular

eat   _____   _____   regular or irregular

write   _____   _____   regular or irregular

fish   _____   _____   regular or irregular

Fill in a progressive form of these verbs: ride, run.

The boys were _____ fast. The girls have been _____ for hours.

Write the progressive form of these verbs: win, swim, rub, bake, pull, look, dance.

_____

Forming Verb Tenses Activities

1. Ask the students to write down everything they did so far today. Example: *woke, washed, dressed, ate, brushed teeth and hair* . . .

2. Read the lists and explain that all the verbs they wrote are in the past tense because they already happened. Explain that the present tense tells about something that is happening now, and ask them to write short sentences giving the present tense of five verbs on their list. Give an example: *I wash my hands before I eat.*

3. Ask students if they think all verbs make the past tense in the same way. Refer them to their lists. Do the verbs *wash* and *eat* make the past tense in the same way? Using as many examples as it takes, lead the students to verbalize that some verbs make the past tense by adding *d* or *ed* and some change their spelling.

4. Explain that verbs that add *d* or *ed* to make the past are regular verbs and those that make the past in a different way are irregular verbs. Post a list of irregular verbs where the students can see it. Ask if the students can add any to the list. Review how irregular verbs form the past and give examples: *run, ran; sleep, slept; go, went; eat, ate* . . . . Some even stay the same: *read* and *read.*

5. Practice making past tense verbs; point out that they must double the last letter of a verb that ends in a consonant: *nap, napped* and *fan, fanned.*

6. Ask what they think future tense means – anything that will happen in the future. Ask them to change several verbs to the future tense: *will wake up, will wash* . . .

7. Ask students to verbalize how irregular verbs make the future tense. It's the same as regular verbs.

8. Review present, past, and future by calling out verbs in one of the tenses and having students call out the word in the other two tenses.

9. Tell the students that progressive verbs end with *ing* and tell us that actions are going on right now. Progressive verbs need a helping verb. Examples are *waking, eating, washing.* If a verb has a short vowel, the ending consonant must be doubled before adding *ing: run, running; win, winning.* If a verb ends with an e, the e is dropped before adding *ing: like, liking.*

10. Ask a student to pantomime an action while others write a progressive verb to describe what she is doing.

11. Review the handout before assigning.

Student Handout 12 Forming Verb Tenses

Name _____ Date _____

Verbs describe action or a state of being. Every complete sentence must have a verb. There are regular verbs and irregular verbs.

You add *d* or *ed* to regular verbs to tell what happened in the past. (past tense)

Irregular verbs follow no set rule for forming the past tense of the verb.

Fill in the blanks below with the past tense of the regular and irregular verbs.

I ride my bike everyday. Yesterday I _____ my bike.

I fall down everyday. Yesterday I _____ down.

I scrape my knee when I fall. Yesterday I _____ my knee.

I am not happy when I fall. Yesterday I _____ not happy when I _____.

What does the future hold for this bike rider? All verbs make the future tense the same way. I will ride. I will fall. I will not be happy.
Go on with the story in the future tense.

I _____ _____ my bike tomorrow. Probably I _____ _____

and I _____ _____ my knee. That's life!

Progressive verbs show that action is progressing or going on right now. Progressive verbs end in ing. Three ways to make progressive verbs are to add ing to the verb (ticking), omit the ending letter e and add *ing* (making), and double the last consonant and add *ing* (running). Finish the story with progressive verbs.

Here are some changes I will be _____ . I will be _____ knee pads.
                                                    make   wear

A helmet will be _____ on my head. I may be _____ all the time, but I will
                        sit   fall

not be _____ myself.
          hurt

Lesson 10 Present, Past, and Future Perfect Verbs

Present, Past, and Future Perfect Verbs
Teacher Information

Note: For younger students, the emphasis should be on using the helping verbs when they use a word like eaten, done, gone, etc., not on the names of the different tenses.

Using the Helping Verbs

There are three "perfect" tenses of verbs that use the helping verbs *have, has*, or *had*: the present perfect tense, the past perfect tense, and the future perfect tense.

Present Perfect: The present perfect describes something that started taking place in the past and is still going on. It uses the helping verb *have* or *has*.

> I *have* dressed like this all my life. (past form)

> She *has* been dressing like this all her life. (progressive form)

Past Perfect: The past perfect describes something that happened in the past and uses the helping verb *had*.

> I *had* dressed like that for a long time. (past form)

> I *had* been dressing like that for a long time. (progressive form)

Future Perfect: The future perfect tense uses *will have* with the past or progressive form of the verb and describes something that will be completed in the future.

> I *will have* cooked for 10 days by the time vacation ends. (past form)

> I *will have* been cooking for 10 days by the time vacation ends. (progressive form)

✓ Present, Past, and Future Perfect Verbs
Pre and Post Test

Which of these verbs are helping verbs? Circle all the helping verbs.

have   go   drive   will   have   am   has   held   end   had

Fill in the helping verbs.

Present Perfect: I _____ studied for the test for the past three hours.

Past Perfect: I _____ studied for two days before today.

Past Perfect: She _____ studied with me.

Future Perfect: I _____ _____ studied for three days by the time I take the test.

Rewrite the four sentences above using the progressive form of the verb.

_____

_____

_____

_____

Present, Past, and Future Perfect Verbs Activities

1. List things that have been going on in school for some time and are still occurring like studying, doing homework, erasing blackboards, shelving books, etc. Tell the students that the present perfect tense of verbs helps express the idea that something that was started in the past is still going on. The helping verbs *have* or *has* help express the idea. Give several examples: *I have taught school for a long time. She has gone to school for years.* Then ask the students to make up sentences using the list items.

   Example: *I have studied math since first grade. Sid has taken karate lessons for a long time.*

2. When something occurred in the past but is not happening now, we use the past perfect tense and the helping word *had*. Give examples. *I had gone to visit my friend before she told me she didn't like me.* Ask students to give examples from their lives.

3. When something has been going on for some time but is going to stop in the future, we use the helping words *will have* to express that idea. *I will have taught 50 years when I retire this spring.* Ask students to think of sentences that tell about things they have been doing but will stop soon. Example: *I will have taken violin lessons for 10 years when I switch to the guitar.*

4. Explain the progressive form of all perfect tenses. Dictate sentences to the students with verbs in the present, past, and future perfect tenses and ask them to write the same sentences in the progressive form. Examples:

   Present: I have worked as a chef for many years.
   I have been working as a chef for many years.

   Past: He had wandered around the country for 10 years.
   He had been wandering around the country for 10 years.

   Future: I will have studied Spanish for 10 years by the time I graduate from school.
   I will have been studying Spanish for 10 years by the time I graduate from school.

5. Review the student handout before assigning.

Student Handout 13 | Present, Past, and Future Perfect Verbs

Name _____   Date _____

The present perfect tense of verbs tells about things that happened in the past and are still happening, like going to school. It uses the helping verbs *has* and *have*.

The past perfect tense tells about things that happened in the past but are not happening now, like using a pacifier. It uses the helping verb *had*.

The future perfect tense tells about things that happened in the past and are ending, like going to elementary school. It uses the helping verbs *will have*.

Fill in the following sentences with your personal information.

I have _____ for a long time. (still happening)

I had _____. (not happening now)

I will have _____ for _____. (happening but will end)

What helper will you use? Depending on the tense, fill in *have*, *has*, *had*, or *will have*.

I _____ eaten my supper before mom came home. (not happening now)

Ken _____ won 30 prizes by the end of the year. (happening but will end)

Jane _____ always been a good student. (still happening)

James _____ been the champion speller for our school. (not happening now)

Our teacher _____ done her best to teach us this year. (happening but will end)

Draw two pictures. One will show something you have done for a long time and are still doing and the other will be of something you no longer do. Write a sentence for each using the progressive form of the verb. Remember the progressive form ends with an *"ing."* Example: I have been running for years.

_____

Lesson 11 Active and Passive Verbs

Active and Passive Verbs Teacher Information

Active and Passive Verbs

Each verb tense can be either in the active voice or the passive voice. In the active voice the subject performs the action; in the passive voice the subject receives the action.

Active Voice

When the subject of a sentence does something, the verb is active.

The children jumped over the fence.

The artist painted a beautiful landscape.

Passive Voice

When the subject of a sentence has something done to it, the verb is passive.

The *fence was jumped* by the children.

The beautiful *landscape was painted* by the artist.

Using the Active or Passive Voice

Using the active voice of a verb makes writing more interesting and moves the action along. Use passive voice if there is no other way to express a thought, for instance when the writer does not know who performed the action. Example: *The tree was cut down.*

Agreement

Verbs must agree in number with the subject of the sentence: The girl goes, the girls go. Sometimes there are words that come between the subject and the verb that lead to confusion about which verb to use. *John*, like many of his friends, *likes* to ski. The *beating* of the drums *was* loud. Therefore, it is important to identify the noun that is the subject of the sentence before deciding which verb to use.

✓ Active and Passive Verbs Pre and Post Test

Change the following sentences from passive to active.

Timmy's shirt was muddied by his slide into home base.

_____

I was awakened by the sun shining through the window.

_____

A promise was given to me by my best friend.

_____

Underline the subject of each sentence. Then fill in the verb that agrees with the noun or nouns in the subject.

Paulo and Marisa _____ the fastest runners in our class. (are, is)

The number of students in our school _____ growing fast. (are, is)

Pots and pans _____ in many different sizes. (come or comes)

The contest, just like all the contests before it, _____ hard to win. (were, was)

Active and Passive Verbs Activities

1. Ask the students to tell what they do when they are active. Make a list of the verbs they use.

2. Explain that being passive is the opposite of being active. Just sitting around and letting things happen to you is a good example to use.

3. Tell them that verbs are active and passive too. Each verb tense can be either in the active voice or the passive voice. In the active voice the subject performs the action; in the passive voice the subject receives the action.

4. Give an example of a sentence written in the active and then the passive voice using some of the verbs they listed. Example: *Sarah lost her purse. The purse was lost by Sarah.* Ask which sentence sounds better to them. The active voice is usually more fluid.

5. Dictate several short sentences to the students in the passive voice and then ask them to write them in the active voice.

6. Discuss why the subject of the sentence must agree with the verb in number and give several examples both of simple sentences and those that have other nouns between the subject and the verb. Remind students that, to find the noun that is the subject of the sentence, they must find the naming word that does or receives the action.

7. Take sentences from a student text and read them incorrectly, using a verb that does not agree in number with the subject. Ask students to find the sentence on the text page and read it correctly.

8. Review the student handout before assigning.

Student Handout 14 | Active and Passive Verbs

Name _____ Date _____

Verbs can be active or passive. Active verbs perform an action; passive verbs show that the action is being done to someone or something.

Active: Jane won first place.   Passive: First place was won by Jane.

Writing, just like life, is much more interesting when there's action.
Use active verbs whenever possible. Change these sentences from passive to active.

The apple was eaten by the hungry boy. _____

The ice cream that we ate was made by two fellows named Ben and Jerry.

_____

The lovely table was designed by the carpenters at the Wood Shop.

_____

Verbs must agree with the noun in the subject of the sentence.
A girl *hurries*.   People *hurry*.   John sees his *friends* and *runs*.   John and Perry *run*.
Fill in verbs that agree with the subject and that make sense in the spaces.

fly/flies float/floats is/are seem/seems don't/doesn't
pull/pulls break/breaks   blow/blows

Two boys _____ a kite in the park. The kite, just like all kites, _____ higher

and higher. The kite _____ striped, red and yellow. Soon it_____ to be just a

speck in the bright blue sky. The boys _____ on the string as hard as they can.

Snap! The string _____ and the kite _____ away.

your turn **Your turn.** On the back of this paper write a poem or story about your favorite animal. Use active verbs and make sure each verb agrees with its subject.

Name _____ Date _____

Here is list of regular and irregular verbs in the present tense. Write the past and future tenses and the progressive form for each verb.

Present	Past	Future	Progressive
walk			
jump			
like			
run			
wake			
sit			

Tell whether the verbs in the following sentences are transitive or intransitive.

Mickey hit a homerun his first time up at bat. _____

The crowd cheered him. _____

He was very proud of himself. _____

Unfortunately, he slipped coming into home base. _____

He broke his ankle. _____

He felt very sad. _____

His father bought him some new books to read while his ankle mended. _____

Which of the above verbs are also linking verbs? Write them here. _____

Use these helping verbs to write three sentences: *am, is, are, was, were, be, been, do, does, did, have, has, had, will, shall, can, may, must, would, should,* and *could.*

Complete each sentence with one of these helping verbs: *is, had, has, will have.* Then tell whether the sentence is in the Present Perfect, Past Perfect, or Future Perfect Tense.

Maria _____ always been afraid of ghosts. _____

She _____ been frightened once when she was very young. _____

Her dad _____ trying to help her get over her fear. _____

By the time Maria is 12, she _____ _____ been to 20 counselors. _____

She _____ tried to conquer her fear for a long time. _____

Change these sentences from the passive voice to the active voice.
Their third period class was skipped by John and Tomas.

_____

The school play was written by Mrs. Gomez's class.

_____

Write your own sentence in the active voice.

_____

Circle the verb that agrees with the subject of each sentence.
Pedro study/studies every night. He want/wants to make his parents proud.

His mother and father want/wants him to be a doctor.

Medicine, out of all possible careers, offer/offers the best chance to help others.

Lesson 12 Adverbs

Adverbs Teacher Information

Definition
An adverb is a part of speech that modifies (describes) a verb, an adjective, or another adverb. Examples: In the phrase "slept soundly," *soundly* modifies the verb *slept;* the *too* in "too hungry" modifies the adjective *hungry; very* in "very quickly" modifies the adverb *quickly.*

Adverbs answer the questions *How? How much? When? Where?*

How? She patted the baby *gently.*
Examples: *carefully, nicely, orderly, patiently, quickly, rapidly, slowly, tiredly, weakly.*

How much? I was *completely* fooled by his lame excuse.
Examples: *less, most, much, entirely, mildly, thoroughly.*

When? I visit my old teacher *occasionally.*
Examples: *always, before, never, often, once, eventually, frequently.*

Where? She lives *upstairs* from my parents.
Examples: *around, here, in, out, there, through, under.*

Some words used as adverbs can be prepositions when they begin a prepositional phrase like *in the house, through the door, under the table.*

Making Adverbs
As you can see from the examples above, some adverbs do not end in *ly* although many adverbs can be made by adding *ly* to an adjective. If an adjective has two or more syllables and ends in a *y*, drop the *y* and add *ily* to make the adverb.

Examples: *careful* to *carefully; nice* to *nicely; quick* to *quickly; weak* to *weakly, shy* to *shyly, angry* to *angrily, happy* to *happily.*

Alternative to Using Adverbs
A descriptive verb rather than a verb plus an adverb makes for tighter writing. He *ran quickly* to me. He *sped* to me.

✓ Adverbs Pre and Post Test

Use these adverbs in sentences:

carefully _____

entirely _____

eventually _____

there _____

What question does each word answer? *where, how much, when, how*

carefully _____ entirely _____ eventually _____ there _____

Change these adjectives to adverbs:

nice _____ poor _____ entire _____

happy _____ sly _____ angry _____

Change these sentences so you do not have to use an adverb.

Mother walked very quietly out of the baby's room.

_____

The baby cried loudly when her mother left the room.

_____

Adverbs Activities

1. Discuss what adverbs are and how they function.

2. Write a list of adjectives and ask students to make adverbs by adding *ly*. Point out that if an adjective ends with a *y* and has two or more syllables, they must drop the *y* and add *ily*. Use adjectives that can be pantomimed like *quick, polite, rude, careless, happy, angry,* and *shy* to make *quickly, politely, rudely, carelessly, happily, angrily,* and *shyly* on the board. Play charades. Students can act out an adverb until classmates guess which adverb they are portraying.

3. Call out a verb to the students so they can respond with appropriate adverbs. Example: *ran (quickly, clumsily, gracefully . . .)*

4. Using some of the combinations from number three, see if the students can convey the same meaning without using an adverb. Example: *sped* could take the place of *ran quickly, grinned* instead of *smiled widely.*

5. Discuss the adverbs that answer the questions how much (*less, most, much, entirely, mildly, thoroughly*); when (*always, before, never, often, once, eventually, frequently*); and where (*around, here, in, out, there, through, under*).

6. Ask students questions that they must answer with adverbs that tell how much, when, or where.

7. Have a contest to see who can find the most adverbs in a fictional story in a specific number of minutes.

8. Review the student handout before assigning.

Student Handout 15 | Adverbs

Name _____ Date _____

Adverbs are words that answer the questions *How? How much? When? Where?*

How? *quickly;* How much? *most;* When? *often;* Where? *here.*

I *often* do *most* of my homework *quickly* right *here* in school.

Fill in the blanks with adverbs to tell us something about yourself.

I _____ do _____ of my homework.
　　when (always, never, eventually)　　　how much (most, much, all, none, some)

My friends think I am _____ wacky.
　　　　　　　　how much (completely, entirely, mildly)

My parents _____ scold me _____.
　　when (often, never, frequently)　　　　　　how (quietly, loudly, unhappily)

Add *ly* to adjectives to make some adverbs. Drop the y and add *ily* to adjectives with two or more syllables that end in y. (quiet to quietly; angry to angrily) Don't use these adverbs too often; use an action verb instead. *walked quietly = tiptoed.* Change the following sentences. Drop the words in *italics* and use one word instead.

The racers *ran quickly* around the track.

_____

The teacher told the class to *speak quietly.*

_____

Max and Manuel crept down the *poorly lit* hallway.

_____

Make adverbs from these adjectives: *happy, kind, shy, quick, nice, wrong, angry.*

Lesson 13 Complements

Complements Teacher Information

A complement is a word that completes the meaning of the subject and verb. Direct objects, indirect objects, predicate nominatives, and predicate adjectives are complements. They all occur in the predicate part of the sentence.

Direct Objects

Direct objects are naming words. Direct objects follow action, transitive verbs. Direct objects answer the questions "whom or what" after the verb.

Juan	finished	the race.
who	did	what
subject	verb	direct object

What did Juan finish? He finished the race. *Race* is the direct object.
A direct object must be a person or thing that tells who or what received the action.

Indirect Object

An indirect object is a noun or pronoun. An indirect object follows an action verb. An indirect object answers the questions "to whom," "for whom," "to what," or "for what."

Juan	gave	his mother	a hug.
who	did	to whom	what
subject	verb	indirect object	direct object

To whom did Juan give the hug? He gave it to his mother. "His mother" is the indirect object.

Predicate Nominative

A predicate nominative is a noun or pronoun. It follows a linking verb. A predicate nominative renames the subject of the sentence.

Mr. Gold	is	a teacher.
subject	verb	predicate nominative

"Teacher" is a noun that renames Mr. Gold and follows the linking verb "is."
Not all linking verbs take predicate nominatives; some take predicate adjectives.

Predicate Adjective

A predicate adjective is an adjective that follows a linking verb. A predicate adjective tells something about the subject.

Mario	is	happy.
subject	linking verb	predicate adjective

"Happy" is an adjective that follows the linking verb *is* and tells something about Mario.

☑ Complements Pre and Post Test

Underline and tell what complements you find in the following sentences.

Gordon's mother gave him a ride to the beach. _____

Gordon finished his sand castle in time to enter the beach contest. _____

Gordon is an expert builder. _____

He was happy when he won. _____

Fill in the correct words in the following sentences.

a linking verb   a noun or pronoun   an action verb

Predicate nominatives and predicate adjectives follow _____.

Direct and indirect objects follow _____.

A predicate nominative is _____.

Complements Activities

1. Review what the students have learned about nouns and verbs by putting several sentences on the board that contain, besides the subject and verb, a direct object. Example: *Carla donated her old computer*. Ask the students to identify the subject and the verb.

2. Then ask the students to read the remaining words in the sentences and ask them what they think those words do. They should determine that "computer" answers the question, "What did Carla donate?"

3. When the students have come to that conclusion, explain that part of speech is called a direct object and discuss the four requisites: it must be a noun or pronoun, it must be in the predicate, it must follow an action verb, and it must answer the question "What" or "Whom."

4. Ask the students to tell about one of their activities by making up short sentences that include a noun, verb, and direct object, and ask other students to verify that the word used for direct object meets all criteria. Is it a noun or pronoun? Is it in the predicate? Does it follow an action verb? Does it answer either what or whom? Example: *I can play the guitar*. Guitar is a noun, it is in the predicate, it follows the action verb "play," and it answers the question, "What can I play?"

5. Practice identifying the direct object by writing more sentences on the board or by finding sentences in textbooks.

6. Follow this same procedure for indirect object, predicate nominative, and predicate adjective.

Student Handout 16 | Complements

Name _____ Date _____

Complements are words that complete the meaning of the subject and the verb. Some complements are direct and indirect objects, the predicate nominative, and the predicate adjective.

True or False?

All complements must be in the predicate part of the sentence. _____

All complements are nouns or pronouns. _____

Direct and indirect objects follow action verbs. _____

Predicate nominatives and adjectives follow linking verbs. _____

All sentences have a direct object. _____

Direct objects (d.o.) answer the questions whom or what.

Fill in a direct object: Harry practices _____ every night.

Indirect objects (i.o.) tell "to or for whom" or "to or for what." Fill in an indirect object:

He made a promise to _____ that he would be the best he could be.

Predicate nominatives (p.n.) rename the subject. Fill in a predicate nominative:

Now he is a good _____.

Predicate adjectives (p.a.) tell something about the subject.

Harry feels very _____ of himself.

In the following sentences, put d.o., i.o., p.n., p.a. over the correct words.

Terri plays the game very well.   She is very talented.

She is a champion chess player.   The chess master awarded her a gold medal.

49

Name _____ Date _____

Adverbs answer the questions how, how much, when, and where. Underline the adverbs in the sentences below and tell what question they answer.

The box is here. _____?

I frequently visit my aunt in Philadelphia. _____?

My dog, Fritz, waits patiently for his food every morning. _____?

I'm not entirely sure how to work this math problem. _____?

My mother says I always embarrass her at the store. _____?

Jose put the dishes down on the table carefully. _____?

The grocery store is near. _____?

Jan was completely surprised by the birthday party. _____?

Change these adjectives to adverbs.

nice_____   angry _____   gleeful _____

wide _____   bad _____   dead _____

It's best to replace some verb and adverb combinations with an action verb. What action verbs could replace the following verbs and adverbs?

smiled widely _____   ran quickly _____

spoke quietly _____   swallowed hastily _____

looked hastily _____   walked heavily _____

What part of speech is the underlined word in each sentence: the direct object, indirect object, predicate adjective, or the predicate nominative?

The children played <u>tag</u> all day. _____

My father is a <u>teacher</u> at my school. _____

Melissa felt <u>sad</u> when she missed the bus. _____

Pierre gave <u>me</u> a ticket to his concert. _____

Draw a line to the correct definition.

Direct objects   rename the subject.

Indirect objects   follow an action, transitive verb.

Predicate adjectives   tell something about the subject.

Predicate nominatives   answer to or for whom or what.

Lesson 14 Prepositions

Prepositions Teacher Information

Prepositions are words that show the relationship between words in a sentence. They act with nouns and pronouns to form prepositional phrases.

Prepositional Phrases

The ball is *on the table*. *On* links ball with table. *On the table* is the prepositional phrase. *After the game*, we went for ice cream. The word *after* shows the relationship between going for ice cream and going to the game. *After the game* is the prepositional phrase. Prepositional phrases do not have a verb.

Punctuating Prepositional Phrases

Usually, if a prepositional phrase comes at the end of a sentence there is no comma; when it starts a sentence, a comma separates it from the rest of the sentence. If there are two introductory phrases, they are followed by commas. A comma may also be used for clarity. The dog went wild *with joy*. *For a surprise,* we had brought him a treat.
On Wednesday, after school, we went to karate class.

Most Common Prepositions

Here are some of the most common prepositions: *above, after, around, at, before, below, beside, between, by, down, during, except, for, from, in, inside, into, near, off, on, over, since, through, to, under, until, up, with, without.*

Prepositions at the End of a Sentence

One common error that both students and adults often make is to end a sentence with a preposition. Sometimes it seems unavoidable because not doing so makes the sentence seem very formal, but try to avoid it as much as possible.

Examples: *Where is the house at*? should be *Where is the house?*
Who was the party for? could be *Whose party was it?*

✓ Prepositions Pre and Post Test

Add a preposition to the following sentences.

We went for ice cream _____ the game.

We ordered sundaes_____ the waiter.

_____ a whole hour, we waited for our ice cream.

Which of these sentences needs one or more commas?

Throughout the whole school year we will have many tests.

We will have many tests throughout the whole school year.

For the whole school year through all kinds of weather Jorge walked three miles to school.

Look through any of your books and find three sentences that have a prepositional phrase in them. Copy them here.

_____

_____

_____

Prepositions Activities

1. Discuss what prepositions are and how they function in a sentence. Emphasize there are no verbs in a prepositional phrase. List the common prepositions on the board.

2. Ask students to look around the room and tell where objects are by saying a sentence that uses a preposition. Example: The clock is *above* the chalkboard.

3. Write sentences on the board that are examples of those that use a comma and those that don't. Point out when commas are and are not needed.

4. Ask everyone in the class to choose a partner. Ask one partner to write four sentences that begin with a prepositional phrase. The second partner must then change the four sentences so that the prepositional phrase ends the sentence. When they complete the task, they should stand. Check sentences together.

5. Review the student handout before assigning.

Student Handout 17 | Prepositions

Name _____ Date _____

⭐ Prepositions are words that show how the subject relates to other words in the sentence. They begin groups of words called prepositional phrases.

In the following sentences, underline each propositional phrase and insert commas where needed.

On the table under the mat was a letter for Anna.

The train was roaring through the tunnel.

After we made cookies we gave some to all our neighbors.

I didn't like what I saw in the bag.

Throughout the entire day Marge was complaining about her sore leg.

Without any help by herself Jenna fixed the flat tire.

For the price of a movie ticket Peter mowed his neighbor's lawn.

Authors use many prepositional phrases in their writing to help readers better understand the meaning of their stories or articles.

Look through a few pages of any story. Find at least five prepositional phrases and write them here.

_____

Your turn!

Write a short story. Underline all the prepositional phrases in your story and be sure to add commas where needed.

_____

_____

_____

_____

_____

_____

_____

_____

Lesson 15 Conjunctions

Conjunctions Teacher Information

Four Kinds of Conjunctions

Conjunctions are words that connect other words or groups of words in a sentence. There are four kinds of conjunctions: coordinating, correlative, subordinating, and linking adverbs.

Coordinating conjunctions join single words or phrases that are alike grammatically. Some coordinating conjunctions are *and, but, or, for, so, yet.*

Ana *and* Jose are here. The conjunction *and* connects two nouns.

We went fishing, *but* we didn't catch anything. The conjunction *but* connects two clauses.

Correlative conjunctions are used in pairs. Some correlative conjunctions are: *either/or; neither/nor; both/and; not only/but also; whether/or.*

I want *either* the ice cream *or* the cake. I want *both* the ice cream *and* the cake.

I want *neither* the liver *nor* the onions.

Subordinating conjunctions connect subordinate clauses with main clauses, groups of words with a subject and a verb. A main clause can stand by itself; a subordinate clause cannot. The conjunction can come between the clauses or at the beginning of the sentence. Some subordinating conjunctions are *after, because, if, since, till, when, where, while.* The subordinate clause is italicized in these sentences.

I will go to the movies *if you will go.*

After I ask my mom if I can go, I'll let you know what she says.

We were late to the show *because Sally couldn't find her wallet.*

While we were waiting for our tickets, the movie started.

Notice if the subordinating conjunction begins the sentence, a comma separates the two clauses.

Subordinating Conjunctions as Prepositions

Some subordinate conjunctions can also be prepositions. If a word introduces a group of words that does not have a subject or predicate, it is a preposition. If it introduces a group of words that does have a subject and predicate, it is a subordinate conjunction.
After school, we went home. In this sentence, *after* is a preposition.
After the school bell rang, we went home. Here *after* is a subordinate conjunction.

Linking adverbs join and show the relationship between two independent clauses, two groups of words that could stand alone as sentences. A semi-colon is used to separate the two clauses with the linking adverb placed in the second clause. The linking adverb is usually followed by a comma. Some linking adverbs are *however, instead, meanwhile, otherwise, still, therefore, nevertheless, thus.*
I ate the liver; *therefore,* I was sick.

My mother knew I would get sick; *nevertheless,* she made me eat the liver.

✓ Conjunctions Pre and Post Test

Fill in appropriate conjunctions.

Ben _____ Jerry wanted to open an ice cream store.

_____ Ben _____ Jerry had ever made ice cream.

They learned all about ice cream _____ they were working in other stores.

Friends told them they would fail; _____, their dream came true.

Write four sentences using conjunctions from this list.

either, or	but	because	while	after	neither, nor

Fill in a linking adverb.

I wanted to go to the store; _____, it was closed for the holiday.

Our car was damaged in the wreck; _____, we had to walk.

Conjunctions Activities

Note: Younger students do not need to know the names of the four kinds of conjunctions. It is enough that they know some words are used as connecting words and they are called conjunctions.

1. Discuss coordinating conjunctions and their function. List on the board: *and, but, for, nor, or, so, yet.* Give some examples of how to use conjunctions and ask the students to make up some sentences linking people, objects, or activities at school. Examples: *At twelve o'clock, we go to lunch and have recess.* (two phrases)

   I think Stan or Laurie will win the race after school. (two names)

2. Discuss the correlative conjunctions that come in pairs. List some things that seem to naturally go together like peanut butter and jelly, socks and shoes, cake and ice cream, hamburger and French fries. Ask the students to make up sentences using the correlative conjunctions and the pairs on the board.

   Examples: *I want neither new socks nor new shoes. I want either the ice cream or the cake.*

3. List some subordinating conjunctions. Make up phrases beginning with a subordinating conjunction and ask students to finish the sentence.

   Example: Teacher: *"Because you have finished all your work."* Student: *"We can have an extra recess."*

4. Ask students to make up phrases beginning with subordinating conjunctions and have them call on other students to finish the sentences.

5. Discuss linking adverbs and the punctuation needed. Write a few sentences on the board as examples.

6. Dictate several sentences to the students using linking adverbs.

   Example: *My family planned a picnic for Sunday; however, the rain spoiled our plans.*

7. Review the student handout before assigning.

Student Handout 18 | Conjunctions

Name _____ Date _____

Conjunctions are words that connect words, groups of words (phrases), or parts of sentences that have a noun and verb (clauses).

Coordinating conjunctions connect similar words and phrases.
Here are some coordinating conjunctions: *and, but, for, nor, or, so, yet.*
Fill in words or phrases so that the sentences make sense.

Petra _____ I went to the movies. We wanted to see Batman _____

Superman II. We got to the theater in time, _____ neither movie was showing.

We didn't want to go back home, _____ we went to the zoo instead.

Correlative conjunctions come in pairs: *either/or; neither/nor; both/and;*
not only/but also; whether/or. Tell how you feel about the following things by
choosing a pair of correlative conjunctions to fill in the blanks.

I'd like to have _____ a pair of stilts _____ a pogo stick.

I like _____ the movies _____ television.

Subordinating conjunctions: *after, because, if, since, till, when, where, while.*
They connect two clauses in a sentence. Fill in subordinating conjunctions below.

I will tell you my name_____ you tell me yours. _____ you tell me, I'll tell you.

Linking adverbs link two sentences: *however; therefore; nevertheless.*
Finish the sentences using linking adverbs.

I found a dog; _____, Dad said I couldn't keep him. I begged and begged;

_____, Dad finally said the dog was mine. The dog made a lot of work for me;

_____, I really love him.

Lesson 16 Interjections

Interjections Teacher Information

Listen! Interjections are words that catch readers' attention because they express emotions like sadness, excitement, dread, fear, or surprise. Exclamation points can separate interjections from the rest of a sentence or, if the writer wants to express a more subdued emotion, a comma separates the interjection.

Examples

Ouch! That really hurt.

Oh, I'm sorry I stepped on your foot.

Commonly Used Interjections

ah	help	oops
awesome	hooray	ouch
congratulations	hurry	outstanding
cool	my goodness	ugh
gee	never	well
good	no	whoops
good grief	no way	wow
great	oh	yikes

Usually interjections are used only in informal writing such as personal letters, fiction, and advertisements.

☑ Interjections Pre and Post Test

Add an appropriate interjection to the following sentences.

_____! I will not do the dishes!

_____! That hurt!

_____! You look great!

_____! We're going to crash!

_____! You did a great job.

Tell what the purpose of an interjection is.

_____

_____

_____

Interjections Activities

1. Discuss what interjections are and how they are used.

2. Start a list of common interjections on a poster and ask students to add any others they use or have heard.

3. Ask students to tell about any times they may have used an interjection.

4. Divide the students into small groups and give them a time limit to write as many sentences that include an interjection as they can. Share some of the sentences.

5. Write a short sentence on the board and ask students to choose an appropriate interjection to accompany it.

   Example: Sentence: *I dropped the glass.*

   Possible interjections: *Whoops! Oh, no! Yikes! Oops!*

6. Review the student handout before assigning.

Student Handout 19 | Interjections

Name _____ Date _____

An interjection is a word used to get someone's attention. Either a comma or an exclamation point can separate the interjection from the rest of the sentence.

Hey! Are you listening to me?
Good grief! You let the cat out!
Whoops! That's the end of that vase.
Yes, I'll go to the dance with you.
Congratulations, you won.

Fill in an appropriate interjection with punctuation in the following sentences.

_____ I found the lost treasure!

_____ I need to tell you something important.

_____ This classroom is too noisy.

_____ Looks like I got paint all over the new couch.

_____ I'll never tell you the secret.

Your Own Personal Interjections
Make a list of interjections you use or hear like *cool, man, yo* . . .

_____

Now write five sentences using the interjections from your list.

_____

_____

_____

_____

_____

On the back of this paper, draw a picture illustrating one of your sentences.

Review, Lessons Twelve through Thirteen

Name _____ Date _____

Prepositions introduce prepositional phrases. Circle all the prepositions in the following sentences and underline the prepositional phrases.

Our family is going to move to a city that is near the ocean.

We will be able to swim in the ocean and speed over the waves in our motorboat.

I am going to learn to scuba dive so I can see what's deep under the water.

After we get settled, I will ask you to visit with us at our new home.

Place commas where needed in the following sentences.

Before we start packing we have to clean our old house thoroughly.

Mom will call the movers after we are done cleaning.

Next week after the movers drive off with our stuff we will drive away too.

Fill in conjunctions in each sentence.

Jorge _____ Pedro are the best football players on our team.

Jorge is taller, _____ Pedro is faster.

_____ Jorge _____ Pedro will get the top athlete award this year.

_____ Jorge's parents _____ Pedro's parents will be able to attend the award ceremony as it is for students only.

_____ Jorge_____ Pedro want to win the award very much.

Draw a line to the subordinating conjunction that best fits each sentence.

I will give you a gift _____ you give me one   while

I'll give you yours _____ you give me mine.   if

Do you want to wait _____ we go home?   after

Let's exchange gifts _____ we eat a snack.   until

Are the italicized words prepositions or subordinate conjunctions?

We can go *in* the morning. _____

We can go *when* we get up. _____

We are not going anywhere *until* noon. _____

We are not going anywhere *until* we do the dishes. _____

Finish these sentences using the linking adverbs nevertheless, however, and therefore.

Ted wanted to go to the concert; _____, his dad wouldn't give him any money.

Ted needed ten dollars; _____, he asked his neighbors if they had any work for him.

Only one neighbor hired Ted; _____, he earned enough for the ticket.

Fill in an interjection with appropriate punctuation at the beginning of each sentence.

_____ I'm going to fall off the wall.

_____ I can't go to the show tonight.

_____ Annabel, you did a super job in the play.

_____ I think that's the end of that lamp.

SECTION TWO
Punctuation

sentence
comma
apostrophe
colon
semicolon
quotation marks

Lesson 17 Sentence Beginnings and Endings

Sentence Beginnings and Endings Teacher Information

Beginnings
The first part of this lesson is simple. Sentences always begin with a capital letter.

Endings
A sentence can end with a period, an exclamation point, or a question mark.

The Period
A period shows the reader that a thought has been completed. It comes at the end of a statement, a command, or a request. Periods are also used in abbreviations. (Mrs. or St.)

I like to ski. (statement)   *Go home*. (command)   *Please take my hand*. (request)

Exclamation Point
Exclamation points are used to get the reader's attention. They show excitement, fear, or some other heightened emotion. It is best not to overuse the exclamation point although advertisers use it quite a bit.

The airplane is crashing!   *The dog bit me*!   *Sale ends tomorrow*!

Question Mark
A question mark is used to end a direct question. You can use a question mark or a period to end a request. *Are you going? Will you please pass the peas? Would you sit down?* *(See Lesson Twenty-Three for more information on sentences.)*

✓ Sentence Beginnings and Endings Pre and Post Test

Rewrite the following sentences correctly.

are you going _____

please pass the peas _____

the ship is sinking _____

Dorothy met a wicked witch _____

can we watch television a little longer _____

Write one statement, one question, one sentence that shows emotion, and one command.

_____

_____

_____

_____

_____

Sentence Beginnings and Endings Activities

1. Point out that a sentence always begins with a capital letter.

2. Explain or review the three marks that are used to end a sentence.

3. Ask the students to divide a piece of writing paper into three equal sections and write one ending mark on each piece of paper. As the teacher calls out sentences, students must hold up the proper ending mark.

4. Have a relay race. Divide the class into groups of four students each. A few groups at a time can participate. Dictate a short declarative sentence. The first student writes the sentence on the board. The second student changes the sentence to a question. The third adds to and changes the sentence so it expresses some emotion. The fourth writes a command. Example: *I'm going to take a make-up test. Am I going to take a make-up test? The teacher is making me take a make-up test! Take the test.*

5. Review the student handout before assigning.

Student Handout 20 | Sentence Beginnings and Endings

Name _____ Date _____

Sentences always begin with a capital letter.

There are three ways to end a sentence: A period ends a statement; an exclamation point ends a sentence that shows emotion like excitement, fear, or anger; and a question mark ends a sentence that asks a question. You may use a period or a question mark to ask someone to do something.

Correct the following sentences.

a) are you coming to see me race _____

b) I'll come if my mom says I may _____

c) wow you really ran fast _____

d) are they going to give you a medal _____

Here's a story that is all mixed up with no capitals and no marks ending sentences. Decide where the capitals and end marks go so the story makes sense.

there's a haunted house on the top of the hill an old man lived there at night you can see lights in the windows of the house do you think it's the old man looking for his dog the dog went away one day and never came back before the old man died he told his son that he would stay in his house until the dog came back oh, that house gives me the shivers

Change these sentences so you have to use a different end mark.

I have to go home. _____

Are you here for the party? _____

Oh, no! I lost your present! _____

Lesson 18 The Comma

The Comma Teacher Information

Commas are one of the most used and misunderstood punctuation marks. They provide a chance for a short pause between words, adding to the clarity of sentences.

When to Use a Comma

Direct Address When you address someone or something, the name of the person or thing is set off by one or two commas, depending on its place in the sentence.

Anne, can you go swimming? I told you, Anne, you have to ask your mother.

Words in a Series Commas separate all words or phrases in a series except for the last one. *I want ice cream, cake, punch, and candy for my birthday party.*

We'll play games, tell stories, and watch a magician do his tricks at the party.

Independent Clauses When two or more independent clauses (mini-sentences) are joined by *and, but, or, nor,* or *for,* use a comma before the conjunction. If the clauses are short, no comma is needed.

My horse won the race easily, and the judges hung a garland of roses around its neck.

I thanked the judge and he congratulated me.

Introductory Phrases or Clauses

Use a comma to separate an introductory phrase from the rest of the sentence.

When I saw that my horse had won the race, I jumped up and down with joy.

Between Consecutive Adjectives

Use commas to separate consecutive adjectives if the word *and* could be used.

The energetic, experienced teacher instructed the class in the martial arts.

Extra Material

Use commas to separate unnecessary information that you insert into a sentence.

The horse, born in August, is only two years old.

We are proud of him, of course, and will race him as long as we can.

Incidental Use of the Comma

Commas are used to separate parts of dates and addresses and in letters after the salutation and closing.

The party will be on August 23, 2007, at my house.

If the year is not included, no comma is necessary.

The party will be on August 23 at my house.

I live at 1820 Happy Drive, Albuquerque, New Mexico.

In letters: *Dear Mrs. Partygoer,*   *Sincerely,*   *Very truly yours,*

When Not to Use a Comma

Never put a comma between the subject and verb of a sentence.

Doing homework every night is very hard.

Never insert a comma when there is only one subject for two phrases joined by a conjunction.

Jeremy insists that he has time to do homework and to play basketball every night.

✓ The Comma Pre and Post Test

Insert commas if they are needed.

Stacy clean the erasers put them back on the board and go to your seat.

Last night while I was sleeping I dreamed about skiing down a huge mountain.

I live at 420 Temple Drive Alamo New Mexico.

John and Pedro like to go to the movies.

Our school built in 1902 is very old but it is very well-kept and beautiful.

Dear Mrs. Kelly I cannot come to the party tomorrow. Yours truly Mary Beth

We will have oranges apples pears and bananas in the fruit salad.

The humorous well-dressed woman addressed the assembly.

The Comma Activities

1. Point out that a comma is used directly after addressing someone. Practice saying aloud sentences that use direct address. Use the word "comma" where it should be inserted. Example: *Mrs. Sanchez, (comma) may I go home now? Jim, (comma) sit down.*

2. Demonstrate how commas are used to separate items in a series. Ask students to think of five or more things they would like to receive for gifts. Then have them write a sentence starting with, *"The gifts I would most like are a guitar, a . . ."* Exchange papers to check correct placement of commas.

3. Explain that a comma separates two independent clauses or two mini-sentences joined by a conjunction. Dictate a few sentences. Example: *Ari wanted to ski, and Kerry wanted to stay in the lodge. The cat wanted to catch the mouse, but the mouse got away.*

4. Give some examples of introductory clauses at the start of sentences. Ask the students to make up some sentences beginning with an introductory clause and tell where the comma goes.
   Example: *Because I was late, (comma) my dad grounded me.*

5. Give examples of sentences where consecutive adjectives should be separated by a comma.

6. Ask students to look through any text or fiction book to find examples of how a comma is used and give the reason for its use.

7. Emphasize that commas are not used to separate a subject and predicate.
   Example: *Juan and Carla went to the store and bought presents for the family.*

Student Handout 21 | The Comma, One

Name _____ Date _____

Commas are used when addressing someone. *Ann, I like your hat.*
Write two sentence addressing two different book characters using their names
in the sentences.

_____

_____

_____

Commas are used to separate items in a series. *I have a pencil, a pen, and a book.*
Put commas in where they belong in the sentence below. Then write your own sentence
telling about several things you or some friend or family member owns or can do.

Tomas can juggle an apple an orange a banana and a mango all at the same time.

_____

_____

When two or more independent clauses (mini-sentences) are joined by *and, but, or,*
nor, **or** *for,* **use a comma before the conjunction. If the clauses are short, no comma**
is needed. Put commas where they belong below.

I wanted to swim longer but my dad said I had to get out of the water.

The temperature had dropped and I was shivering from the cold.

It was late and Dad was mad.

I couldn't find my towel so I dried off by rolling in the sand.

Use a comma to separate an introductory phrase from the rest of the sentence.

Add commas and finish the sentences below.

When the school bell rang _____

After I fell off the bike _____

Student Handout 22 The Comma, Two

Name _____ Date _____

⭐ **Use commas to separate unnecessary information inserted into a sentence.**
Add commas where needed in the sentences below.

I stood up of course when they called my name.

I didn't after all know what they wanted.

It was I thought very strange that I was singled out.

It was for a good reason luckily and not because I had done something wrong.

Use commas to separate parts of dates and addresses and in letters after the salutation and closing.
Insert commas where needed.

I live at 220 Happy Lane Sharpsville New York.

The new school rules will take effect on Monday January 15 2008.

Dear Marty I can go camping with you and your family. Your friend Santo

Commas separate consecutive adjectives when the word *and* would be appropriate.
We accepted many gifts from the generous kind woman.

Your turn. Insert commas and finish the letter below with your teacher's name, your personal likes and dislikes, and your signature.

Dear

My favorite subjects this year are

_____ _____ and
_____. On the other hand I don't particularly enjoy _____ or
_____. I enjoyed the field trip on Monday February 5.

Your student

Lesson 19 The Apostrophe

The Apostrophe Teacher Information

Uses of the Apostrophe
Apostrophes are used to

1. show possession (*Marty's towel*);

2. form contractions (*isn't, won't*); and

3. make the plural of lower case letters and words used as words. (*g's, and's, but's*)

Possessive Singular Nouns
When making the possessive of a singular noun or an indefinite pronoun, add *'s* even when the word ends with an *s.*

driver's license	cook's apron	James's book	the boss's focus
anybody's license	no one's apron	someone's book	everybody's focus

If a singular noun has more than one syllable and ends with an s, add only an apostrophe.

Business' finances   mattress' firmness   sourpuss' attitude

Possessive Plural Nouns
To make the possessive of a plural noun, add *'s*. If the word ends in s, add only an apostrophe.

children's pets   women's hats   workers' pay   cars' tires

Individual and Joint Ownership
If two people own one thing, only the second name gets an *apostrophe s.*

John and *Linda's* house is up for sale. (Only one house is owned by both people.)

If each person named in the sentence owns his own thing, both names get an *'s.*

John's and *Linda's* houses are up for sale. (They each have a house.)

Contractions
Apostrophes take the place of some letters in order to shorten words for a more informal way of communicating.

aren't = are not	*can't = cannot*	*couldn't = could not*	*didn't = did not*
don't = do not	*hadn't = had not*	*haven't = have not*	*shouldn't = should not*
wasn't = was not	*won't = will not*	*it's = it is*	*they'll = they will*
she'll = she will	*he'll = he will*	*they're = they are*	*I'll = I will or I shall*
we're = we are	*who's = who is*	*Mary's going. = Mary is going.*	

Plurals
Apostrophes are used to make the plural of words used as words and lower-case letters. Examples: How many *and's* are in this sentence? There are five *m's.*

☑ The Apostrophe Pre and Post Test

Insert an *apostrophe* or an *apostrophe s* where they are needed in the sentences.

Bella homework was too hard for her.

Juan slept at his grandparents house last night.

We went for a ride on Mr. and Mrs. Jones sailboat.

Jess and Tony cars are going to be in a race at the Speedway.

There are too many ands in this sentence.

My brothers going to be a football player for the Jets.

Write the contractions for the following words.

cannot	do not	will not	would not
it is	it will	they will	have not
we are	they are	had not	who is

Write a sentence about something a friend owns. Use a possessive noun.

_____

The Apostrophe Activities

1. Some of the information covered in this lesson has been partially covered in Lessons Three and Six, so the students should be familiar with some of the uses of the apostrophe.

2. Review how to use an apostrophe when forming contractions. Write *are not, cannot, could not, did not, do not, had not, have not, should not, was not,* and *will not* on the board. Make up a sentence using a contraction and ask the students to write the contraction next to the words it replaces. Example: *I haven't any money.* Student writes *haven't* next to *have not.*

3. Dictate short sentences using *is* and *are*, and then dictate the same sentence using *is* and *are* contracted with nouns. All students write on paper while one or two write the sentences on the board for comparison. Example: *My sister is a nurse. My sister's a nurse.*

4. Call out sentences that name people and their possessions. Students, in turn, must say the person's name and the possession using a possessive noun.
   Examples: Teacher: *Jean has a guitar.* Student: *Jean's guitar*
   Teacher: *Bob and Mary have a monkey.* Student: *Bob and Mary's monkey*
   Teacher: *Raul and Sandy each have a car.* Student: *Raul's and Sandy's cars*

5. Review the difference between possessive pronouns and contractions.

Possessive Pronouns	Contractions
its	it's (it is)
their	they're (they are)
whose	who's (who is)

6. Write *it's, its, they're,* and *their* on four separate places on the board. Call out sentences using those words; students must go stand by the correct word and explain why they chose that word. This activity is easier to do with a few students at a time.

7. Explain that apostrophes are used to make the plural of lower-case letters and words used as words. Give examples.

8. Review student handout before assigning.

71

Student Handout 23 | The Apostrophe

Name _____ Date _____

Use apostrophes to show possession (Maria's towel).

Look around the room. Write the names of three people you see and something they own. Use an apostrophe to show they own the item.

1._____

2._____

3._____

Use apostrophes to make the plural of lower-case letters and words that are used as words. (No if's, and's, or but's, you are grounded. There are three a's, two b's, and five m's.)

Put apostrophes where they belong.

The word Mississippi has four ss and two ps.

You have used too many ands in your story.

Write a sentence using at least one plural of a letter, or a word used as a word.

_____

Use apostrophes to make contractions like can't and I'll.

Answer these questions in the negative. Use contractions.

Are they going to the store?_____

Is your grandfather the king of England?_____

Will you do a favor for me?_____

"It's" is a short way to say "it is." "Its" shows possession.

Fill in it's or its.

_____ my fault you fell down.

The monster showed _____ huge fanged teeth.

The movie was so bad, _____ review advised against seeing it.

Review, Lessons Seventeen through Nineteen

Name _____ Date _____

All of the sentences in the following conversation need ending marks, and some of them also need commas. Add the correct punctuation to each sentence.

Mom: *Stop listening to that loud music and go rake the leaves in the yard*
If you don't do your work, I'll have to take away your allowance
I'm getting mad

Daisy: *Oh Mom did you say something to me I couldn't hear with these earphones on*

Mom: *As you can see the yard is covered with red green orange and yellow things called leaves and leaves must be raked and loaded into trash bags*

Daisy: *You don't have to use silly unkind sarcasm with me*
As soon as I put my earphones away I'll rake the leaves

Mom: *Thank you*

Write your complete address here. Then write today's date including the year.

_____

_____

Draw a line to the correct word for each sentence.

The dogs like _____ new canned dog food.   it's

_____ going to get this food from now on.   you're

_____ more expensive than the dry mix.   their

I think _____ very generous.   your

You are good to _____ dogs.   they're

Add apostrophes where needed.

Marthas boat is docked at the towns marina.

Can you guess the boats name?

The name has four ss and two ps in it.

The name is the same as a states name.

Its Mississippi.

The marinas owner says there are no ifs, ands, or buts about it; Martha will win todays race.

Write a short story using contractions for at least five of the following:
cannot, do not, will not, I will, you will, they will, I am, we are, they are, it is.

Rewrite the sentences using contractions.
Example: Jean is going to the store. Jean's going to the store.

I think she will buy dessert for dinner. _____

Maybe Jean will buy a pie. _____

I would like that. _____

Jean is a considerate person. _____

Lesson 20 Colons and Semicolons

Colons and Semicolons Teacher Information

Colons

Colons introduce a list or series.

Here is what you need to bring to camp: towels, bedding, snack food, clothing for three days, and a flashlight.

We visited three national parks: Yellowstone, the Grand Canyon, and Carlsbad Caverns.

Colons are used to write time in numbers. You do not have to use the words o'clock after the number.

3:00 in the afternoon   12:00 midnight   2:00 A.M.

Often colons are used instead of a comma in the greeting of a business letter.

Dear Mr. Smith: To All Students: Attention Comic Book Collectors:

Semicolons

- Use a semicolon between two independent clauses that are related in thought and are not joined by a conjunction. *Mary left her sweater at camp; it was torn and dirty.*

- Use a semicolon between clauses that are joined by a linking adverb like however, therefore, moreover. *Mary's mother was upset about the sweater; however, she said she would buy her a new one.*

- Use a semicolon between clauses that have another form of punctuation within the clause. *Mary wants a blue, a green, and a pink sweater; when she goes shopping with her mother, she will ask for all three.*

- Use a semicolon to separate a series of items if the items contain other punctuation. *Mary and her mother will go to Blue Villa, a boutique; Nickel's, a department store; and Wally World, a discount store.*

✓ Colons and Semicolons Pre and Post Test

Use a colon or a semicolon where needed.

We are leaving for our field trip at __**100**__. (1 o'clock)

Here is what you need to bring suntan lotion, a wide brimmed hat, a towel, and a bathing suit.

Last year, some students forgot bathing suits they didn't get to go on the beach.

Students must follow certain rules no running, no leaving the group, and no swimming far from shore.

Students not following these rules will be sent home moreover they will be suspended from school for 10 days.

The class will be visiting the beach, the water slide park, and the cafeteria we will spend about one hour at each place.

Colons and Semicolons Activities

1. **Colon:** Show what a colon looks like and explain its several uses: to introduce a list or series after a complete sentence; to write time in numbers; and in the greeting of a business letter.

2. Brainstorm a list of healthy lunches the students would like to see served in the school cafeteria. As a class, draft a letter to the principal. Use the colon in the greeting as well as in the list of items the students would like to see served.

3. Ask the students questions about school that need to be answered with the time written using a colon. Example: *What time does school start? What time do we have PE?*

4. Dictate the following letter for practice using a colon three different ways.

    Dear Mr. Baskin-Robbins:

    I think you should have more than 31 flavors of ice-cream. These are some flavors you might want to invent: Cookie Coconut, Lemon Licorice, (ask the students to make up a few more names of flavors they might like), and Grape Gorilla.

    Also it would be good if your store had longer hours. You could be open from 9:00 in the morning to 11:00 at night.

    Thank you for taking the time to read my letter.

    Yours truly,

5. Review the colon handout before assigning it.

6. **Semicolon:** Put two sentences on the board showing how to use semicolons.

    Pat broke his violin; he lost his temper and threw it on the floor.

    Pat's teacher was very upset; therefore, she gave Pat a week's detention.

7. Ask the students to write a two sentence story that uses both rules. Share the stories.

8. Write the example given in the teacher information of clauses that have another form of punctuation within the clause: *Mary wants a blue, a green, and a pink sweater; when she goes shopping with her mother, she will ask for all three.* Using this sentence as a skeleton, ask students to make up sentences. Example: *Tony wants to go on the Ferris Wheel, the roller coaster, and the daredevil jump; when he goes to the fair, he will spend all his money on these rides.*

9. Write a sentence on the board that demonstrates how to use a semicolon when there is a series of items containing other punctuation. Ask students to write sentences using this rule and this sentence as a frame. *I want ham, lean and fat-free; eggs, over easy; and toast for breakfast.*

10. Choose several students to dictate their sentences to the class and correct together.

11. Point out to the students that all of the above sentences could be two separate sentences but are more fluid written as one.

12. Review semicolon student handout before assigning.

Student Handout 24 | Colons

Name _____ Date _____

Colons introduce a list or series.

Rewrite the sentences, inserting a colon and commas.

a) We ate five different desserts candy cake pie pudding and ice cream.

_____

b) I like several animals at the zoo bears giraffes elephants otters and tigers.

_____

Colons are also used in writing the time of day.

Answer the questions by writing a time using a colon.

What time do you get up in the morning? _____

What time does school start? _____

When does school get out? _____

What is the time of your favorite TV show? _____

What time do you go to bed? _____

What time do you go to sleep? _____

Use both of the rules in this sentence.
Rewrite the sentence putting in colons where they are needed.
I have to take my medicine four times each day 800, 1200, 400, and 800.

_____

When writing business letters, use a colon after the greeting of the letter.
Write a short business letter to your teacher, your parents, or someone else about something that concerns you. After the greeting, use a colon instead of a comma. Use a clean piece of writing paper so, if you like, you can actually send the letter you write.

Student Handout 25 | Semicolons

Name _____ Date _____

Use a semicolon to separate two independent clauses, two groups of words that could be sentences all by themselves, that are related. *I have a cat; I also have a dog.*

Write a sentence with two clauses telling two related facts about yourself. Use a semicolon to separate the clauses.

_____

_____.

Use a semicolon to separate clauses that are joined by a linking adverb. *My cat is friendly; however, my dog is a menace.*

Write two clauses joined by a linking adverb. Use a semicolon.

_____

Semicolons separate clauses that have another form of punctuation within the clause. *I have red, blue, and green shoes; they match my new jeans.*

Write a clause that uses commas, then another clause that is related. Use a semicolon.

_____

Semicolons separate series of items that have commas within the series. *I want a puppy, a beagle; a cat, a Manx; and a bird, a parakeet.*

Put the semicolons in the right places.

On our trip, we went to Disneyland, an amusement park to Speedway, a race course and to Universal Studios, a movie studio.

Lesson 21 Quotation Marks

Quotation Marks Teacher Information

Quotation marks are used in several different ways.

Direct and Indirect Quotes

Quotation marks make a fence around someone's exact words, direct quotations.

Mary said, "I love my new sweaters. Thank you."

You do not use quotation marks when you are explaining what someone said, indirect quotes.

Mary said she loved her sweaters and thanked her mother.

Terms

Quotation marks can be used around expressions or terms to emphasize them.

Tina told her friends she was "happy as a clam."
You need to "boot up" the computer now.

Titles

Use quotation marks with titles of magazines, articles, poems, reports, short stories, and songs.

We sing "The Star Spangled Banner" every day at school.
I wrote a poem called "Sing, Sing, Sing."

Punctuating with Quotes

Commas and Periods Always place commas and periods inside quotation marks.

"I want to go home," she said.   *"Take me home."*

Question Marks and Exclamation Points Question marks and exclamation points can be placed inside or outside the quotation marks.

If they are part of the quote, they go inside.
If they are not part of the quote, they go outside.

I absolutely love the article "Teen Town Tunes"! (not part of quote)
"Come and get it!" he yelled. (part of quote)
Have you seen the movie, "Finding Nemo"? (not part of quote)
My favorite book is "Where is Harvey?" (part of quote)

Semicolons and Colons

Semicolons and colons are always placed outside quotation marks.

I read "Moby Dick"; it was a great book.
We saw so many animals in the movie "Alaska Wonderland": polar bears, seals, walruses, and, believe it or not, insects.

Quotation Marks Pre and Post Test

Put quotation marks where they belong.

Petra said, I practiced my violin for so long, my fingers turned blue.

The comic was so funny I laughed like a loon.

Our school song, Hail Central High, is really great.

Barry asked, Would you like to go see a movie?

I liked two things about the movie Pride and Prejudice: the beautiful scenery and the main character.

Is your favorite book Moby Dick?

The book I like is Jane Eyre; it's one of my favorites.

✓ Quotation Marks Activities

1. Explain that quotation marks can be used in several different ways: to show that someone is speaking, to emphasize phrases, and for the names of written works like books and songs.

2. Distribute newspapers or magazines and pair students to try to find an example of each way to use quotation marks. They can cut out the examples, paste them on a piece of drawing paper, and label to show what use they illustrate.

3. Ask students to look at their examples and tell the class where the punctuation is placed in each sentence. As the students share their sentences, the teacher writes the rules that apply on a piece of tag board so they can be posted for future reference.

4. If the students miss any rules for punctuating with quotation marks, fill in the gaps by giving examples and writing the rules on the tag board.

5. Write a classroom story. Use quotation marks in all three ways. Include enough sentences so that all punctuation rules are covered. Ask students to check the list of rules to make sure the story is punctuated correctly.

6. Dictate a list of book and song titles and a few sentences using quotation marks.

7. Review each handout before you assign it.

Student Handout 26 | Quotation Marks

Name _____ Date _____

Direct and Indirect Quotes

Quotation marks make a fence around someone's exact words.
This is called a direct quotation. *Jean said, "I have to go home. It's late."*
You do not use quotation marks when you are explaining what someone said.
This is an indirect quote: *Jean said she had to go home because it was late.*

Some of these sentences need quotation marks and some do not. Add quotation marks where they belong.

Dad said that my dog had to stop barking so much.

He's bothering all the neighbors, he said.

He added, You'd better train him or out he goes.

I said that I would do my best, but this dog has a mind of his own.

Terms and Titles

Quotation marks can be used around terms like "dead as a doornail" to emphasize them and for titles of magazines, articles, poems, short stories, TV shows, and songs.

Where can you use quotations in the sentences below?

I went to see Cinderella last night. It was a great movie and I felt as happy as a lark when I went home. My mom was reading The Princess Diaries and Dad was watching Law and Order on television, so they never even noticed I had come home. That burst my bubble.

> **Indirect quotes do not use quotation marks.** On the back of this paper change the next two sentences into indirect quotes and finish the story.
> Jean said, "I want to get a German shepherd." Dad answered, "The biggest dog we will have is a beagle."

Student Handout 27 | Quotation Marks Punctuation

Name _____ Date _____

⭐ Commas and periods go inside quotation marks.
"Hi," she said. "My name is Faye."

Question marks and exclamation marks go inside the marks if they are part of the quote and outside if they are not part of the quote.
Do you like the movie "Superman"?   "You're really pretty!" he said.

Rewrite these sentences. Make sure the quotation marks are in the right place.

Did you ever read the book Old Yeller? _____

She said I'm really scared! _____

He said Don't you want to see the movie? _____

I'm going to the library now called Margaret _____

_____

Semicolons and colons are always placed outside quotation marks.
We played lots of games on the ship "Sarah Dawn": shuffleboard, golf, and tag.
We wanted to see the movie "Spiderman"; Dad said we couldn't go. ⭐

Insert the colon or semicolon in the right place.

My favorite colors are in the crayons made by Crayola magenta, chartreuse, and teal.

There are lots of animals in the Jungle Book I like the apes the best.

I went to the library to check out the novel Old Yeller it was checked out already.

My favorite movie is Scream! it is very scary.

---

your turn | **Your turn:** Pretend you are talking to your friends. On the back of this paper, write four sentences that show what you are saying. Use quotation marks.

Name _____ Date _____

Rewrite the times below using colons.

Midnight _____   nine o'clock _____   three o'clock _____

You are writing a letter to your friend. Show two ways you can punctuate the greeting.

_____   _____

Insert a colon or a semicolon in the following sentences.

Mr. Rigatoni owns the tire factory in town he invited us to come see how tires are made.

I have three favorite sports basketball, football, and soccer.

On our trip we will visit Santa Fe, the capital of New Mexico Austin, the capital of Texas and Oklahoma City, the capital of Oklahoma.

Bruce is a great chess player he is the champion of every chess tournament.

Three foods make me break out in hives peanuts, sesame seeds, and broccoli.

Tomas wants a football, a fishing rod, and a new book when it's his birthday, he'll ask for all three things.

Graciela is very close to three people in her family her uncle, Pedro Gomez her aunt, his wife and Rosa, their daughter.

Put quotation marks in the sentences where they are needed.

Jane said I want to go to the seashore.

Do you want to go on the merry-go-round? asked Mrs. Schmidt

I didn't know how to boot up the computer, so I asked my friend Penny.

The book I am reading, My Friend Flicka, is about a horse.

The poem, Trees, by Joyce Kilmer is my favorite.

Did you like the movie March of the Penguins? she asked me.

How are you doing? asked Mary.

I'm so excited! said David.

I am absolutely crazy over the song Here's My Heart!

First we're going to see the movie Sounder; then we'll read the book.

I have two favorite parts in the movie King Kong: the part where you first see him and the part where he wipes the tears from the girl's face.

Answer this question. Why don't these sentences need quotation marks?

_____

Petra said that she liked the gift Sally gave her.

Mr. Small told Jim to rewrite the essay by Monday.

Change one of them so it does need quotation marks.

_____

Putting It All Together

subjects
predicates
phrases
clauses
modifiers
run-ons &
fragments

Lesson 22 Sentences

Sentences Teacher Information

A sentence is a group of words that expresses a complete thought. In order to express a complete thought the sentence must have a **subject and a verb**.

A subject is a person or thing that performs an action. The **verb** is the action performed.

Beginnings and Endings
Sentences always begin with a capital and end with one of three end marks: a period, a question mark, or an exclamation point.

Kinds of Sentences
There are four different kinds of sentences:

A **declarative sentence** makes a statement. It ends with a period.
After the table is cleared, we are going to play a game.

An **imperative sentence** gives a command. It can end with a period or a question mark.
Please clear the table. Would you please clear the table?

An **interrogative sentence** asks a question. It ends with a question mark.
Why do I have to clear the table?

An **exclamatory sentence** shows emotion or gives emphasis to the words spoken. It ends with an exclamation point.
I'm tired of clearing the table every night!

☑ Sentences Pre and Post Test

Underline the subject and circle the verb in the following sentences.

Tammy wants to go shopping. Her mother thinks she should do her homework instead.

Put the correct punctuation at the end of these sentences and identify what kind of sentence each is, giving the correct name for each.

We're going to crash   _____

I am going home now   _____

Will you go with me   _____

Open the door   _____

Write four complete sentences: one that gives a statement, one that gives a command, one that asks a question, and one that shows some sort of emotion.

_____

_____

_____

_____

85

Sentences Activities

1. Discuss the four types of sentences. List their names on the board.

2. Practice identifying the types by giving examples of each and asking students to tell what kind of sentence each example is.

3. Ask each child to write four sentences, one of each kind in no set order. Then have them trade papers to try to identify the types of sentences. Allot time for students to discuss whether their partner identified them correctly. Ask some to share the sentences aloud with the class.

4. Call out a type of sentence and ask students to find an example of that type of sentence in a work of fiction.

5. Review the student handout before assigning.

Student Handout 28 | Sentences

Name _____   Date _____

A sentence is a group of words that expresses a complete thought. There are four kinds of sentences: the declarative ends with a period; the interrogative ends with a question mark; the exclamatory ends with an exclamation point; and the imperative ends with a period or question mark. Sentences always begin with a capital.

Place the correct punctuation mark after each of these sentences and then tell what kind of sentence it is.

Jed's going to have a party   _____

Are you going   _____

There's going to be a band   _____

I just can't wait   _____

Go home and get ready   _____

Each kind of sentence has a certain function. In your own words tell what the function of each kind of sentence is.

A declarative sentence   _____

An interrogative sentence   _____

An exclamatory sentence   _____

An imperative sentence   _____

Your turn!
Write a story using all four kinds of sentences in any order you wish as long as it makes sense. Then trade papers with someone and see if they can tell what type each of your sentences is.

Lesson 23 Simple, Complete, and Compound Subjects and Predicates

Teacher Information

Subjects and Predicates

The subject is what the sentence is about. The predicate contains the verb and tells about the subject.

Most of the time, the subject comes first in the sentence before the predicate, but it can sometimes come after it. (Into the storm came *the snow plows*.) In a command, it can be eliminated altogether because the subject *you* is understood. (Wash your hands.)

Simple, Complete, and Compound Subjects

The Simple Subject

The simple subject is a noun or pronoun alone.

The *man* is here.   *He* is here.
The *merry-go-round* broke down. *It* broke down.

The Complete Subject

The complete subject is the noun or pronoun and all words that modify it.

The tall black-haired woman is from New Mexico.
What she told us about her state was interesting.

A Compound Subject

A compound subject is made up of two or more nouns, pronouns, or phrases.

The *man and woman* are from New Mexico.
He and I are going to the dance.
Where you go and what you do are your business.

Simple, Complete, and Compound Predicates

The predicate always contains a verb and, sometimes, it contains direct and indirect objects.

A Simple Predicate

The simple predicate is the *verb* alone: The man *runs*. Runs is the simple predicate.

The Complete Predicate

The complete predicate is the *verb* with all the words that relate to it.

He *won a medal in the race*.

"Won a medal in the race" is the complete predicate.

Compound Predicate

A compound predicate consists of two or more verbs.

He *ran and jumped*.

"Ran and jumped" is the compound predicate.

✓ Simple, Complete, and Compound Subjects and Predicates Pre and Post Test

Circle the complete subject and underline the complete predicate in these sentences. Put an X on the simple subject.

The tall mysterious woman carried a black umbrella and a leather satchel.

A police car followed the woman down the street.

The strange woman walked very quickly. She was soon out of sight.

Which of these sentences have a compound subject and/or compound predicate?

Carla and Sid play basketball together every day. _____

They like to jump for the hoop and slam the ball into the basket. _____

My family picnics and swims in the summer. _____

Juan and Pedro are my good and faithful friends. _____

Simple, Complete, and Compound Subjects and Predicates Activities

1. **Subjects:** Explain the difference between a simple subject (the noun alone – *girl*), a complete subject (the noun with all the words that tell about it – *the tall pretty girl*), and a compound subject (two or more nouns – *the elephant and the giraffe*).

2. Hold up pictures that lend themselves to making up sentences with a simple, a complete, and a compound subject. Example: a picture illustrating the nursery rhyme "Mary Had a Little Lamb" would yield: *Mary* has a lamb – simple subject. *The young girl* has a lamb – complete subject. *Mary and her lamb* like having fun at school – compound subject.

3. **Predicates:** Explain the difference between a simple predicate (one verb – *like*), a complete predicate (*like having fun at school*), and a compound predicate (two or more verbs – *ran and tripped*).

4. Using the same pictures used in number two above, ask the students to make up sentences with both a simple, a complete, and a compound predicate. Mary *loves her lamb*. (There's only one verb so it's a simple predicate containing a direct object) (*Loves her lamb* is the complete predicate – *loves* is the verb and *her lamb* is the direct object.) Mary *feeds and bathes her lamb*. (There are two verbs so it's a compound predicate.)

5. Relay Race for Subjects and Predicates: Have a relay race. Divide the class into groups with four students in each and ask the groups to line up single file in front of the board. Write these directions on the board. "Circle the complete subject. Underline the simple subject. Put two lines under the complete predicate. Put an X on the verb or verbs." Ask the first person in each line to write this sentence on the board. *The children in this class have too much fun.* At the count of three, the relay race begins. The first child follows the first instruction then goes back to her line, hands the chalk to the next student until all instructions are followed with each child performing one task. The team finishing first wins providing they have followed the instructions correctly. Do this several times using different sentences.

6. Review the student handouts before assigning.

Student Handout 29

Simple, Complete, and Compound Subjects

Name _____ Date _____

The simple subject is the noun or pronoun alone.

The complete subject is the noun or pronoun and all words that modify it.

A compound subject is made up of two or more nouns, pronouns, or phrases.

Make up a sentence about a favorite character from a book or movie.
Underline the simple subject. Put a circle around the complete subject.

_____ .

Make up a sentence about two favorite characters. Circle the compound subject.

_____ .

Look at the italicized words in each sentence. Then tell whether they show a simple, complete, or compound subject.

Mary fell down the stairs and scraped her knee. _____

Shari, her best friend, helped her to the nurse's office. _____

The *nurse* told her it was just a scratch and sent her to class. _____

A tearful Mary cried that she wanted to go home. _____

The nurse and her teacher wondered, "Is it the knee or the math test?" _____

Was she hurt or did she want to skip the test was what they wondered. _____

All the children in Mary's class knew she had not studied for the test. _____

Your turn: On the back of this paper, finish the story above with three sentences. In the first, underline the simple subject. In the second, underline the complete subject, and, in the third, use a compound subject and underline it.

Student Handout 30

Simple, Complete, and Compound Predicates

Name _____ Date _____

A simple predicate is the verb only, a complete predicate is the verb and everything that modifies it, and a compound predicate is one that contains two or more verbs.

Fill in the following blanks with something about yourself and circle the correct sentence part.

When I get cold, I _____.   compound predicate

When it's hot out, my family_____.   simple predicate

On Saturdays, I have to _____.   complete predicate

Find three different sentences, at least one with a compound predicate, in a textbook or storybook and copy them here. Then in each sentence, circle the simple predicate in one color, the complete predicate in another color, and a compound predicate in a third color.

_____

_____

_____

_____

Now write a sentence about the colors you used and underline the complete predicate with your favorite color.

_____

_____

Tell whether the italicized predicate is simple, complete, or compound.

Katrina and Josef *went* to the movies.   _____

They *looked for and found* good seats.   _____

They *didn't like the long and boring movie.*   _____

91

Lesson 24 Phrases, Clauses, and Complex Sentences

Phrases, Clauses, and Complex Sentences Teacher Information

Besides subjects and predicates, there are two other building blocks of sentences: phrases and clauses.

Phrases

Phrases are groups of words that do not express a complete thought. They do not include both a subject and a verb.

I bought *a pair of running shoes*. I ran *at the track*. I fell, *hurting myself badly*.

Clauses

Clauses are groups of words that have a subject and a verb.
An **independent clause** can stand alone as a sentence.

Independent clause: *the road was completely blocked*

A **subordinate clause** cannot stand alone as a sentence.

Subordinate clause: *because the snow fell all night long*

Join the independent and the subordinate clauses together to make a complete sentence.
Because the snow fell all night long, the road was completely blocked.

Complex Sentences

A complex sentence will have an independent clause and one or more subordinate clauses. It sounds like complex sentences would all be very long, but they can be quite short.

When it's vacation time, we will go skiing. (1 subordinate and 1 independent)

Punctuating Complex Sentences

If a subordinate clause begins a sentence, it is followed by a comma.

When winter comes, the city's snowplows come out of storage.

If an independent clause begins a sentence, there is no comma.

The city's snowplows come out of storage *when winter comes.*

If a sentence is very short, no comma is needed no matter what begins the sentence.
In winter the plows come out of storage.

✓ Phrases, Clauses, and Complex Sentences Pre and Post Test

Underline the phrases in the sentences below.

I bought a bright red blouse at the store.

I bought it with my birthday money.

Because it's so pretty, I'm going to wear it to the party.

It will go nicely with my orange skirt.

Circle the independent clause and underline the subordinate clause in the sentences.

Wherever the food is, you will find my friend Mr. Santa Claus.

Because he eats so much, he has to go on a diet.

The poor reindeer struggle to pull the heavy load when Santa goes to deliver toys.

Look at the seven sentences above. Put a C after each sentence that is a complex sentence.

Phrases, Clauses, and Complex Sentences Activities

1. Discuss what makes up a phrase. Phrases do not express a complete thought – *at the farm, on the hayride, above the sink.*

2. Look through any written material for examples of phrases.

3. Ask a few students at a time to write short sentences on the board so the rest of the class can pick out the phrases in each sentence.

4. Play a game much like volleyball. Have the students line up across the room from each other. A student on Team A starts a sentence that must be finished with a phrase by another student on Team B. Example: *I won a prize . . . for perfect attendance.* The volley should go back and forth as quickly as possible.

5. Demonstrate the difference between a phrase and a clause: A clause has a noun and a verb just like a sentence. Discuss the two different kinds of clauses: independent and subordinate. Give several examples of each. Look for examples in written works.

6. Point out that when a subordinate clause begins the sentence, there is a comma between the clauses. There is no comma when an independent clause starts a sentence.

7. On separate pieces of paper, write sentences with one independent and one subordinate clause. Cut the sentences in half and distribute them to the class. Ask the students to find the other half of their sentences.

8. Ask each student to write one sentence using both an independent and subordinate clause. Have students exchange papers with a partner who will circle the independent clause and underline the subordinate clause before returning the paper.

9. Dictate several sentences using both types of clauses.

10. Tell the students that they have written complex sentences and explain exactly what that means: a sentence that has both independent and subordinate clauses.

11. Review the handout before assigning.

Student Handout 31

Phrases, Clauses, and Complex Sentences

Name _____ Date _____

**Phrases are groups of words that do not express a complete thought.
Circle the phrases in the following sentences.**

The football game was cancelled because of the snowstorm.

We could not play in the falling snow.

The coaches of the two teams set a new date for the game.

**Clauses are groups of words that have a noun and a verb. Independent clauses
can stand alone; subordinate clauses cannot. Complex sentences have an
independent clause plus one or more subordinate clauses.**

**Finish these sentences and put an I (independent) or an S (subordinate) to show
what kind of clause you wrote.**

When I asked my teacher for less homework, _____.

I really don't like homework _____.

Because I'm good at basketball, _____.

_____, my family goes to the beach.

**When a subordinate clause begins a sentence, a comma separates the clauses.
No comma is used if an independent clause starts a sentence.**

If the sentence needs a comma, insert one.

When I get home after school I feed the dog right away.

My dog is always at the door because he's glad to see me.

Your turn! Use phrases and clauses in a short story about something funny
that happened.

Review, Lessons Twenty-Two through Twenty-Four

Name _____ Date _____

Complete the following sentence.

All sentences must have a _____ and a _____.

Draw lines to the correct answers.

A declarative sentence   gives a command.

An interrogative sentence   makes a statement.

An exclamatory sentence   asks a question.

An imperative sentence   shows strong emotion.

Name each kind of sentence and add the correct punctuation.

Go home now   _____

I'm falling   _____

Why are you mad at me   _____

I live in the United States of America   _____

Underline the simple subject and circle the simple predicate in these sentences.

The tall basketball player scored 20 points in his last game.

The powerful machine plowed the field in no time at all.

Underline the complete subject and circle the complete predicate in these sentences.

My cousin Patsy has a lot of musical talent.

The huge, scary gorilla stood on the top of the Empire State Building.

Combine these sentences into one that has a compound subject.

Paulo ran in the race. Marc ran in the race. _____

Combine these sentences into one that has a compound predicate.

Gerri can swim very fast. Gerri can run very fast. _____

Add a subordinate clause to these sentences.

_____, Maria will go swimming.

Jacob said he wanted to go _____.

Add an independent clause to these sentences.

Until we find out where the party is, _____.

_____ because Janie was grounded.

Circle the phrases in these sentences.

We are going to the movies tonight. I hope we won't be caught in the rush hour traffic. I want to see the beginning of the movie. After the movie, we'll have some ice cream at the drive-in.

Draw a line to complete each sentence correctly.

A subordinate clause   has no subject or predicate.

An independent clause   cannot stand alone in the sentence.

A phrase   has one independent and at least one subordinate clause.

A complex sentence   can act as a complete sentence.

Write a complex sentence. _____

Lesson 25 Using Modifiers

Using Modifiers Teacher Information

Modifiers
A *modifier* can be a single word or a group of words that adds to the meaning of the rest of the sentence.

Exhausted but happy, the skier took first place in the race.
The modifier, *exhausted but happy*, tells us a little more about the skier.

Kinds of Modifiers
Modifiers can follow many different parts of speech.

- Modifiers can follow gerunds, verbs that end in *ing* and act as nouns.

  I like *hiking in the mountains*.

Gerund	Modifier
hiking	*in the mountains*

- Modifiers can be part of participial phrases. A participle is a verb that ends in *ing, d, ed, en, n*, or *t* and acts as an adjective. A participial phrase is the participle plus the modifier.

  Slipping on the ice, Bennie broke his wrist.

Participle	Modifier	Participial Phrase
slipping	*on the ice*	*slipping on the ice*

- Modifiers can be part of an infinitive phrase. An infinitive consists of two parts: the preposition *to* and a verb as in *to eat* and *to swing*. An infinitive phrase is the infinitive plus the modifier.

  John felt like he was going *to be sick*.

Infinitive	Modifier	Infinitive Phrase
to be	*sick*	*to be sick*

Dangling Modifier
The biggest mistake made with a modifier is that it is attached to the wrong word or words in the sentence and becomes what is called a "dangling modifier."

Coming over the hill, the ski slope looked enormous to the skier.
This is an example of a dangling modifier. It sounds like the ski slope is coming over the hill! What a sight to see! Since the skier is coming over the hill, it's more correct to say:

Coming over the hill, the skier thought the ski slope looked enormous.
The importance of teaching modifiers is in recognizing and avoiding dangling modifiers.

✓ Using Modifiers Pre and Post Test

The modifiers in these sentences are not in the right place. First tell what noun they should be modifying. Then rewrite the sentences so they make sense.

Floating high in the sky, the boy saw his balloon fly away.

Cleaning the house, the mop tripped Sandy.

Finishing the snowman, the shovels were tossed aside by the children.

Add modifiers to the sentences to extend the meaning.

The old car, _____, sat waiting for its last drive.

_____, Pedro fell down.

Using Modifiers Activities

1. Discuss what a modifier is: a group of words inserted into a sentence to make the meaning clearer.

2. Give several examples of sentences with modifiers, both oral and written.

    Examples: My grandmother, *80 years old today*, knows a lot of fun games.
    The ship, *old and rusty beyond belief*, sagged under our weight.
    I gave my mother a rosebush, *bursting with pretty pink buds*, for her birthday.

3. Ask students to make up some sentences about objects in the classroom using modifiers.

4. When the students show that they know how to use modifiers correctly, give some examples of dangling modifiers and ask students to tell why the sentences are wrong.

5. Then work on writing the sentences correctly. Example: *Balancing on the surf board, the waves looked huge to Tom.* The modifier is used incorrectly because the waves are not balancing on the surf board. Revision: *Balancing on the surf board, Tom thought the waves looked huge.* The modifier is used correctly because Tom is on the surf board.

Student Handout 32 | Using Modifiers

Name _____ Date _____

A modifier is a single word or a group of words that adds to the meaning of the rest of the sentence.

Jerry's car, *an old clunker*, almost didn't make it all the way home.
An old clunker is the modifier that gives us more information about the car.

Pick three things that you own and write a sentence about each one using modifiers.

_____

_____

_____

The biggest mistake made with a modifier is that it is attached to the wrong word or words in the sentence and becomes what is called a "dangling modifier."

Wrong: Walking on the ice, the wind pulled at Amahl's face.
Better: Walking on the ice, Amahl felt the wind pull at his face.

Fix the following sentences so they don't have dangling modifiers.
Dancing a polka, the dog tripped Jorge.

_____

Wearing the old scarf, the moths' work was evident to Miriam.

_____

Slipping on his boots, the old dog went with Alan for a walk in the rain.

_____

Your turn: Make up a sentence with a dangling modifier and ask a friend to correct it.

Lesson 26 Run-on Sentences and Fragments

Run-on Sentences and Fragments
Teacher Information

Run-on Sentences

Run-on sentences are sentences that do just what their name implies. They run on and on.

This sentence is way too long. It does not give the reader time to pause or take a breath. *The skier wanted to win the race but he stumbled and almost fell as he came over the final slope so he knew he was going to have to ski as fast as he could to make up the lost time, he did, and by trying his hardest he won the race.*

The sentence can be fixed by adding punctuation or by adding or deleting words. Revised: *The skier wanted to win the race, but he stumbled and almost fell as he came over the final slope. He knew he had to ski as fast as he could to make up the lost time, so he did. By trying his hardest, the skier won the race.*

Here's another run-on sentence and a way to change it by adding a semicolon. *Meet me at the game tonight I will be in the right-field stands.* Revised: *Meet me at the game tonight; I will be in the right-field stands.*

Run-on sentences can be avoided by using periods, conjunctions, and semicolons.

Sentence Fragments

Sentence fragments are, just as the name implies, only part of a sentence and do not express a complete thought. They can look like a sentence with punctuation and a capital letter but, if they don't make sense and leave you asking a question, then they are sentence fragments.

Fragment: *When the snow comes.* (Question: What happens when the snow comes?) Sentence: *When the snow comes, we will build a snowman.* (The question is answered.)

✓ Run-on Sentences and Fragments Pre and Post Test

This sentence is a run-on sentence. Break it up into several sentences.

Marc wanted to go to the baseball game very badly but his father told him he had to mow the lawn and wash the car before he could go and even though Marc protested his father would not give in and finally Marc did his work and was able to go to the game.

_____

_____

_____

_____

_____

_____

Put an "SF" after all sentence fragments.

_____ When I went to the party.

_____ I saw my friend there.

_____ He was serving the sodas.

_____ Because I was all alone.

_____ When my mom came to get me.

Run-on Sentences and Fragments Activities

1. Write a lengthy sentence on the board. Ask a few students to read it aloud. Discuss how difficult it is to read and understand because of its length.

2. Ask for suggestions on how the sentence could be made more manageable.

3. Point out the different ways to fix a run-on sentence: using two or more sentences, using a conjunction, using a semicolon.

4. Dictate a run-on sentence to the students and ask them to revise it so it reads more fluently. Share several versions.

5. Discuss sentence fragments and the reason they are not a complete sentence—they leave the reader asking a question. Example: *Because the snake escaped.* What happened because the snake escaped? *Because the snake escaped, my dad said I couldn't have any more pets.* Now the reader knows what happened.

6. Call out some sentences and some sentence fragments. Ask student to differentiate between them. If it is a sentence fragment, ask them to identify the question they are left asking and finish the sentence.

7. Review the student handout before assigning.

Student Handout 33

Run-on Sentences and Fragments

Name _____   Date _____

Run-on sentences are very long sentences that are hard to understand because they are several sentences rolled into one.

Rewrite the following run-on sentence so it makes more sense.

When the television is on it is very hard for me to do my homework because I want to watch whatever is on and so I can't concentrate on what I'm doing sometimes I finish my homework but I don't do a very good job.

_____

_____

_____

_____

Sentence fragments are only part of a sentence and do not express a complete thought. Sentence fragments leave you asking a question.

When Dad comes home.

Question: What will happen when Dad comes home?

Here is a story containing some sentences and some sentence fragments. Change the sentence fragments into complete sentences and punctuate the sentences.

After we painted the dock, we asked Dad if we could go fishing

_____

Before we could fish _____

While we were putting the boat into the water

_____

Finally we put out from shore _____

Looking back at the shore _____

Oh, no! Without our fishing poles _____

"I'm sorry," said Dad. "Maybe you'll have better luck next time"

_____

Review, Lessons Twenty-Five through Twenty-Six

Name _____ Date _____

Tell whether the phrases in these sentences begin with a gerund, a participle, or an infinitive.

Hiking in the woods, I found many leaves.   _____

I felt so happy to be alive.   _____

Caught in the net, the angry fox growled.   _____

The woman wanted the long day to be over.   _____

Running a race is my favorite pastime.   _____

We saw a frightened rabbit hidden by a bush.   _____

These sentences contain dangling modifiers. Rewrite the sentences correctly.

Driving down the mountain, the trees we saw were beautiful.

_____

Sleeping on the bus, the conductor woke the vagrant.

_____

Although they may seem harmless and playful, hikers can be hurt by bears.

_____

Underline the fragments and choose two to rewrite as complete sentences.

Out in New Mexico.

He laughed uproariously at the movie.

Dancing around the Maypole.

Because you left.

Hiking in the mountains is great exercise.

Writing can be hard.

Whenever I do something I shouldn't.

_____

_____

Rewrite these run-on sentences.

Don't worry about Bill, he will be okay, his injury isn't so bad.

_____

I'll be at the game around six o'clock, can you meet me there, we'll have fun watching our team win.

_____

Jill wanted to stay at home and read a good book, she picked out three at the library, she looked forward to a quiet day. _____

_____

Student Handout Table of Contents

1: Common Nouns 5

2: Proper Nouns 6

3: Singular & Plural Regular Nouns..9

4: Singular & Plural Irregular Nouns 10

5: Possessive Nouns 13

6: Personal Pronouns 18

7: Indefinite Pronouns..21

8: Possessive Pronouns 24

9: Adjectives One 27

10: Adjectives Two 28

11: Verbs 33

12: Forming Verb Tenses 36

13: Present, Past, and Future Perfect Verbs 39

14: Active and Passive Verbs 42

15: Adverbs 46

16: Complements 49

17: Prepositions..53

18: Conjunctions..56

19: Interjections 59

20: Sentence Beginnings and Endings 65

21: The Comma, One 68

22: The Comma, Two 69

23: The Apostrophe..72

24: Colons..76

25: Semicolons 77

26: Quotation Marks 80

27: Quotation Marks Punctuation 81

28: Sentences 87

29: Simple, Complete, and Compound Subjects 90

30: Simple, Complete, and Compound Predicates 91

31: Phrases, Clauses, and Complex Sentences 94

32: Using Modifiers 98

33: Run-on Sentences and Fragments..101

Index

A

Active Voice 40
Adjectives 25
   Comparisons.............................25
   Compound 25
   Descriptive 25
   Limiting 25
   Predicate..............................25, 47
Adverbs 44
   Adverb Alternatives 44
   Linking 54
   Making Adverbs 44
Agreement 15, 19, 40
Antecedent...15
Apostrophe 70
   Contractions 22, 70
   Individual Ownership.....................70
   Joint Ownership 70
   Plurals......................................70
   Possessive Plural 70
   Possessive Singular 25
Articles...25
Auxiliary Verbs 31, 37

C

Capitalization 3, 63
   Proper Nouns 3
   Sentences 63
Clauses...92
   Independent 66, 92
   Subordinate................................92
Colon 74, 78
Commas.......................54, 57, 66, 78, 92
Common Nouns 3
Complements...47
   Direct Object 47
   Indirect Object 47
   Predicate Adjective......................47
   Predicate Nominative 47
Complete Predicate 88
Complete Subject 88
Complex Sentence................................92
Compound Predicate 88
Compound Subject................................88
Conjunctions 54, 99
   Coordinating...............................54
   Correlative 54
   Linking Adverbs as.......................54
   Subordinating 54
Contractions 22, 70

D

Dangling Modifiers...............................96
Declarative Sentence 85
Determining Parts of Speech 3
Direct Address.......................................66
Direct Object...47
Direct Quotation 78

E

End Marks for Sentences...............63, 85
Exclamation Point 57, 63, 78, 85
Exclamatory Sentence 85

F

Fragments 99
Future Tense 34
Future Perfect Tense............................37

G

Gerunds 96

H

Helping Verbs (Auxiliary) 31, 37

I

Imperative Sentence 85
Indefinite Pronouns 19
Interrogative Sentence 85
Independent Clauses 66
Indirect Object 47
Indirect Quotation 78
Infinitive Phrases 96
Infinitives...96
Interjections 57
Intransitive Verbs 31
Introductory Phrases/Clauses 66
Irregular Nouns 7
Irregular Verbs 31, 34

L

Linking Adverbs 54
Linking Verbs 31

M

Modifiers 96
    Dangling Modifier 96

N

Nouns 3
    Abstract 3
    Common 3
    Concrete 3
    Irregular 7
    Noun (definition) 3
    Plural Nouns.....................................7
    Possessive.................................11, 70
    Proper Nouns 3
    Regular 7
    Singular Nouns.................................7

P

Participial Phrases 96
Participles 96
Passive Voice 40
Past Tense 34
Past Perfect Tense........................37
Periods.............................63, 78, 85, 99
Phrases..92
Predicates 88
    Complete 88
    Compound 88
    Simple...88
Predicate Adjective..................25, 47
Predicate Nominative 47
Prepositional Phrases 51
Prepositions.............................51, 54
Present Tense...........................31, 34
Present Perfect Tense 37
Pronouns 15
    Agreement 15, 19
    Demonstrative 25
    Indefinite 19
    Me / I 15
    Personal 15
    Possessive...22

Q

Question Mark 63, 78, 85
Quotation Marks 78
    Direct Quotations 78

R

Regular Verbs 31, 34
Run-on Sentences 99

S

Semicolons.............................74, 78, 99
Sentences 63, 85, 99
    Complex 92
    Declarative 85
    Exclamatory 85
    Fragments 99
    Imperative 85
    Interrogative 85
    Punctuation......................................63
    Run-on 99
Series of Words 66
Subjects 88
    Complete 88
    Compound 88
    Simple...88
Subordinating Conjunctions 54

T

Transitive Verbs 31

V

Verbs 31
    Active Voice 40
    Agreement with Subject....................40
    Future Perfect Tense.........................37
    Helping (auxiliary).......................31, 37
    Intransitive 31
    Irregular 31, 34
    Linking 31
    Passive Voice 40
    Past Perfect Tense............................37
    Present Perfect Tense 37
    Progressive 34
    Regular...31, 34
    Tenses..31, 34
    Transitive 31
Voice..40
    Active Voice 40
    Passive Voice 40

9 781586 832131